THE DIVINATORY TAROT

THE DIVINATORY TAROT
Translated by Beryl Stockman

PAPUS

AEON

First published in 2008 by

Aeon Books, Hilltop, Lewes BN7 3HS

Copyright ©2008 Beryl Stockman

The rights of Papus to be identified as the Author of this work have been asserted in accordance with §§ 77 and 78 of the Copyright Design and Patents Act 1988.

All rights reserved. No part of this publication may be reproduced, stored in a retrieval system, or transmitted, in any form or by any means, electronic, mechanical, photocopying, recording, or otherwise, without the prior written permission of the publisher.

British Library Cataloguing in Publication Data

A C.I.P. for this book is available from the British Library

ISBN-13: 978-1-90465-805-4

Typeset by Vikatan Publishing Solutions, Chennai, India

www.aeonbooks.com

CONTENTS

PREFACE	VII
INTRODUCTION	1
CHAPTER ONE The composition of the tarot	5
CHAPTER TWO The seventy-eight tarot cards	7
CHAPTER THREE Drawing and reading tarot cards	169
CHAPTER FOUR Interplay of the cards	193
CHAPTER FIVE Interplay of the arcana and numbers	227
CHAPTER SIX General conclusion	243

PREFACE

Papus was the pen name of Gerard Encausse. Born in Spain on July 13, 1865, of a Spanish mother and a French father, Louis Encausse, a chemist. His family moved to Paris when he was four years old, and he received his education there. As a young man, Encausse spent a great deal of time at the Bibliothèque Nationale studying the Kabbalah, the Tarot, the sciences of magic and alchemy. He was much inspired by the occult writings of Eliphas Lévi, whose translation of the "Nuctemeron of Apollonius of Tyana" printed as a supplement to "Dogme et Rituel de la Haute Magie" (1855), provided Encausse with his nom de plume: "Papus" meaning "physician".

Papus was a member of many esoteric organisations including the Hermetic Brotherhood of Light and the Hermetic Order of the Golden Dawn, as well as being an author of many occult books and articles. Outside of his esoteric activities he was also a spiritual student of the French spiritualist healer Master Philip of Lyon. When World War One broke out, Papus joined the French army medical corps.

While working in a military hospital, he contracted tuberculosis and died on October 25, 1916, at the age of 51.

"Le Tarot Divinatoire: Clef du tirage des Caries et des sorts" published in Paris in 1909 was Papus' last major work seemingly written as a response to R. Falconnier's book "Lames Hermétiques du Tarot Divinatoire" (1896) that detailed divination using only the 22 major arcana of the tarot. This latter book was the first to publish Tarot images explicitly based on the Egyptian style Initiation, published in Paul Christian's "History of Magic". In her ground breaking work "The Underground Stream" Christine Payne-Towler has convincingly argued that these are in fact reproductions of the initiation rituals of The Fratre Lucis a French esoteric organisation.

Several reasons can be posited for why Papus felt strongly enough about Falconnier's book to bring out his own. Firstly was the importance he placed on the minor arcana in divination, Falconnier used only the major. Secondly was his allegiance to the work of Eliphas Levi whose esoteric correspondences to the major arcana differ from those of the Falconnier tarot in minor but significant ways.

The book has received scant attention in the English speaking world. The noted occultist A.E.Waite lists it in the extensive bibliography of his "Pictorial Key to the Tarot" and Mouni Sadhu recommends it in his monumental "The Tarot".

Little is known about the draughtsman, Gabriel Goulinat, whom Papus commissioned to create the cards that illustrate the book. Whether he was a student of the mysteries himself, or working entirely under Papus' tutelage is not clear. The designs are much less stylized than those of Falconnier but feature the same egyptian theme derived from the Fratre Lucis manuscript.

The surrounding correspondences are derived from the work of Eliphas Lévi and Papus' own work. Though most of these correspondences are fairly straightforward however I feel that the Archeometer of Saint-Yves needs further explanation. In 1903 Alexandre Saint-Yves d'Alveydre (1842–1909) published an enormous work intended to assess the real value of each philosophical, scientific or religious system and its place in the universal tree of science or tradition. This system draws upon a series of symbols and interpretations relating to the Ark of the Covenant. Alongside the constellations, planets and musical notes, the most important symbols on the disc of "archéomètre" are the letters of a varied set of alphabets among these are the letters of the Holy Alphabet, reflecting the astral alphabet and it is these that appear on the major arcana.

We have taken some minor liberties in the structure of the book to make it more readable. The most obvious of these is to move the Tarot images from the back of the book to Chapter 2 where Papus obviously intended them to be. We have also taken the divinatory information originally presented in Chapter VI as "Detailed Study of the Divinatory Meanings of the 78 Cards according to Etteila and D'Odoucet" and the descriptions of the cards by Christian found at the end of Chapter V and placed them opposite the relevant card image.

The rest of the chapters are largely made up of various ways of reading the cards. Rather than concentrating on the meanings of individual cards Papus is concerned with the relationships between them in a spread. To this end he includes much material from early writers on the Tarot. Material he felt was often unavailable to the seekers of his period, a concern which is at least as valid now. A note of caution should be sounded here. Much of early French cartomancy was developed from reading a standard pack of cards and a pack in which the pip cards number 2, 3, 4, 5 and 6 have been discarded to give a deck of thirty two (again a significant kabalistic number). Much of the work Papus cites is based on this reduced deck, but once this is understood it in no way detracts from its value for the earnest seeker.

On a final note I would like to give my warmest thanks to the translator Beryl Stockman who, as a labour of love, has made this classic work available to an English speaking audience and in doing so done the whole esoteric community a huge service.

Antony Balfour
London 2008

Introduction

Contemporary researchers into occultism affect a certain disdain for the art of divination. However, studying the temperaments opens the way to some exceedingly valuable medical discoveries, palmistry gives some remarkable insights into the physiology of the great sympathetic nerve, which governs the formation of the distinguishing marks engraved in the skin. But the most fertile ground of all for research is the study of Tarot.

Tarot, Thora, Rota, Athor, a combination of pictures and numbers that is without doubt one of the consummate masterpieces of ancient initiation. Many researchers have found themselves drawn to the idea of studying it.

Over twenty years ago I was fortunate enough to rediscover the general key to the structure of the Tarot, as referred to by Guillaume

Postel and Eliphas Lévi, who did not actually talk about the structure itself. I worked out the structure and determined how it relates to Postel's outline as a whole and how it relates to the Minor Arcana. At this point it is necessary to make a vital observation. The majority of modern occultist writers who deal with the subject of Tarot show intense enthusiasm for studying the Major Arcana and equally intense contempt for any research involving the Minor Arcana, which are the forerunners of our playing cards.

There are even numerous false Tarot interpretation systems based solely on the 22 Major Arcana, and which take no account whatsoever of the 56 Minor Arcana. That is quite simply a puerile approach. The Tarot is a marvellous whole, and the system that applies to the body must apply to the head and vice versa. So it is important to remember that the Minor Arcana are of the utmost importance when studying the Tarot, just as the houses are of crucial importance to the study of Astrology.

In times of antiquity all physical systems of consulting the invisible were composed of two parts. There was a fixed part, normally numeral or hieroglyphic in nature (and often both), and a moving part, which was often hieroglyphic and numeral. In Astrology, the fixed part is represented by the Zodiac and the houses and the moving part by the planets and their aspects. Numbers were attached to each section, and the process of adding or subtracting combinations of these according to the aspects formed the basis of this type of Astrological Onomancy, which is now an almost completely lost art. The popular game of snakes and ladders is an adaptation of Tarot in which the fixed part consists of numbers and hieroglyphs, and the moving numbers produced by the throwing of the dice pass over these.

In Tarot the fixed part takes the form of the four suits of 14 Minor Arcana, each consisting of four face cards: King, Queen, Knight and Page, these being the major cards of the Minor Arcana, and ten numbered cards, going from Ace to Ten.

Tarot lends itself to a host of applications, and like the Ars Magna of Ramon Lull—which is an adaptation of it—makes for the possibility of resolving all major philosophical problems. However, in the case of women who find their curiosity aroused by Tarot, it is not the latter aspect that draws them, so much as the fact that, with Tarot, you can determine certain laws of chance in a way that renders it suitable for divination purposes. You can "draw cards" using Tarot!

A would-be serious writer studying the art of drawing the cards? How absolutely frightful! No study is frightful, and I have learned many curious things through studying divinatory Tarot. Furthermore, I have discovered a few things which will make for a great deal of precision when using the Tarot. For example, by going through the work of the little-known researcher Etteilla, and that of the brilliant clairvoyant Mlle Lenormand, I was able to determine the time attributed by the Ancient Egyptians to each of the cards. So henceforth, this in turn will enable a good reader to predict the time and day when the dark handsome man is likely to meet the pretty blonde widow one night at some point in the future. I can assure you it wasn't easy to find precision in this labyrinth of imprecision, and that is precisely the role of the Minor Arcana in the Tarot. The Minor Arcana add fixity and the notion of time to the general information provided by the Major Arcana. Such was their role in ancient Astrology teachings and such is their role in divinatory Tarot. Even greater precision can be achieved through the use of a numerical astrological table, about which I shall speak at greater length.

PAPUS

CHAPTER ONE

The composition of the tarot

Tarot appears to be a card game. However, it is really a set of hieroglyphics that originated in Ancient Egypt.

I have already dedicated a special volume to the origins and philosophical applications of Tarot (*The Tarot of the Bohemians*). But such considerations are of little use to anyone wishing to use the Tarot to interpret impressions of the past, present or future. So I am going to give as clear an account of the Tarot as possible from a purely divinatory point of view.

The Tarot consists of 78 cards: 56 cards called the minor arcana, from which today's cards are derived, plus 22 other cards, no longer found in card decks, and which are called the major arcana.

The minor arcana are composed of four suits: Wands, Cups, Swords and Coins.

Wands became the Clubs of modern playing-cards, Cups became Hearts, Swords became Spades and Coins became Diamonds.

Each suit consists of 14 cards: the King, Queen, Knight and Page, in other words, the four face cards of the suit (King of Wands, Queen of Wands, Knight of Wands, Page of Wands etc.), plus 10 numbered cards, Ace, 2, 3, 4, 5, 6, 7, 8, 9 and 10, i.e. 14 cards for each of the suits: Wands, Cups, Swords and Coins, making a total of 56 cards in all.

Each of the 56 minor arcana has a divinatory meaning, which must be taken into consideration, and which varies depending on whether the card comes out upright or reversed. In addition to the minor arcana there are 22 cards called the major arcana or trumps, and these indicate major events applicable to nations, social groups and individuals.

It is essential to study the 22 major arcana, particularly if you wish to use the Tarot [for divination purposes], because their equivalents do not exist in today's cards. One aid to such study is to think of the 22 major arcana as being made up of 3 series of 7 cards, numbered from 1 to 21, plus one card—the Fool—which has the number 0, and which comes between the 20th and 21st cards.

Etteilla worked on the above arcana for many years. In order to understand their meanings, see the illustrations further on in this book and study the images one after the other.

CHAPTER TWO

The seventy-eight tarot cards

The Major Arcana are laid out as follows. The hieroglyphic figure, drawn by Gabriel Goulinat, forms the central image. Each of the figures has been reproduced according to information drawn from the most authentic documents I could find.

At the top of the card is the number. Corresponding numbers and symbols in the following alphabets are [arranged in descending order] down the left hand side: 1) Latin; 2) Hebrew; 3) Sanskrit; 4) the corresponding Egyptian symbol; 5) the Watan symbol according to the Archeometer of Saint-Yves d'Alveydres and by special permission of the author. These equivalents will prove invaluable to occultists of all schools and for those seeking knowledge of occult science.

At the bottom of each card is its traditional meaning in large letters, and underneath this, three other meanings: spiritual, moral or alchemical and physical. The latter is the one used for divination. So for divinatory Tarot readings it is sufficient to look at the name right at the bottom of each card.

On the right hand side are the astrological equivalents, which make it possible to determine the day or the month.

THE SEVENTY-EIGHT TAROT CARDS

The Works of Christian, Etteilla and d'Odoucet*

In his book *L'Homme Rouge des Tuileries* (*The Red Man of The Tuileries*), and then in *Histoire de la Magie* (*The History of Magic*), Christian applies the Tarot to onomantic astrology in a rather curious way. Each of the major arcana forms the subject matter of a careful study, one which will of great benefit to all researchers wishing to further their knowledge of the philosophical aspects of Tarot. Therefore, I feel it is necessary to draw the works of Christian to your attention by including his study of the major arcana.

In order to assist the work of true researchers, this chapter also provides a summary of some of the divinatory writings resulting from the arduous tasks undertaken by Etteilla and his follower d'Odoucet.

*Editors Note: In the original work all the Tarot Card images were grouped at the end of the book and the descriptions from Christian and Etteilla were included in a separate chapter. This was almost certainly to do with printing issues and so in this edition I have grouped the images and descriptions for the readers convenience.

The material from the works of Paul Christian appears on the left hand page, followed by the interpretations of Etteilla and d'Odoucet. A further overview of the Major Arcana by Christian can be found on page 54.

Etteilla made major changes to the titles, order and images of the Major Arcana to fit with his own cosmology. Thus the attribution of his divinatory meanings to the traditional tarot images is one of conjecture. Those given here are supplied by Papus. Other attributions have been suggested.

MAGUS, AND SYMBOLISES THE WILL

In the divine world $A = 1$ expresses the absolute Being who contains and from whom comes forth the infinity of all possible things. In the *intellectual world*, it expresses Unity, the origin of action, and in the physical world, it expresses Man, the highest of the relative beings, called upon to raise himself into the concentric spheres of the Absolute through perpetual expression of his faculties.

Arcanum I is represented by the Magician, the model of the perfect man, in full possession of his physical and moral faculties. He is standing upright: the stance of will proceeding towards action. He is wearing a white robe, the image of original or regained purity. His belt is a serpent biting its tail, the symbol of eternity. Around his forehead is a gold band. Gold denotes light, and the circular band is an expression of the continuum in which all created things revolve. In his right hand the Magician holds a golden sceptre, a symbol of authority. He is raising it towards the heavens in a gesture of aspiration to knowledge, wisdom and power. The index finger of his left hand points to the ground, indicating that the mission of the perfect man is to reign over the material world. The dual gesture also expresses the idea that human will ought to be an earthly reflection of the divine will, thus promoting good and preventing evil.

Laid out on a cubic stone in front of the Magician are a goblet, a sword and a gold shekel with a cross engraved in the centre. The goblet signifies the mixture of passions contributing to happiness or misfortune, according to whether we are their masters or their slaves. The sword symbolises labour, the struggle that overcomes obstacles and the tests that pain makes us undergo. The shekel, symbol of a set value, represents aspirations fulfilled, works accomplished, the sum total of power won by perseverance and will-power. The cross, the stamp of the infinite with which the shekel is engraved, proclaims the ascension of this power into the spheres of the future.

Remember, child of Earth, that man should, like God, engage in ceaseless action. To will nothing and do nothing is as fatal as to will and do ill. If the Magician appears among the prophetic signs of your horoscope, this is a sign that a firm will and faith in yourself, guided by reason and love of justice will lead you to the goal you wish to attain and will preserve you from perils along the way.

THE SEVENTY-EIGHT TAROT CARDS   11

A French		Mother Letter
א Hebrew		Centre of the Heavens
ॠ Sanskrit		Visible and Invisible
ו Egyptian		
Archeometer of Saint-Yves	**THE MAGICIAN**	

Principle–Divine Essence
The Earth
The Man–The Father

Etteilla 15. Sickness

Upright: From the point of view of spiritual healing this card means illness, infirmity. Derangement, pain, anxiety, harm or evil, displeasure. Damage, trouble, suffering, punishment or penalty, misfortune, disaster.

Reversed: Mental illness, headache, unfortunate position, disgrace, annoyance, affliction. Doctor, magus

DOOR OF THE OCCULT SANCTUARY, AND SYMBOLISES THE KNOWLEDGE WHICH MUST GUIDE THE WILL

In the divine world, B = 2 expresses the consciousness of the absolute Being, who embraces the three periods of all manifestations: the past, the present and the future. In the *intellectual world*, it expresses the Binary, a reflection of Unity, and knowledge, the perception of visible and invisible things. In the physical world, it represents woman, the matrix of Man, who unites with him to bring about a similar destiny.

Arcanum II is represented by a woman seated between two columns on the threshold of the temple of Isis. The column on her right is red. This colour signifies the pure spirit and its ascension above material things. The column on her left is black, and represents the night of chaos, the captivity of the impure spirit in the bonds of material things. The woman is wearing a tiara with a crescent moon at the top. Underneath this is veil, the folds of which fall over her face. On her breast she wears the Solar Cross, and on her knees is an open book half-covered by her cloak. As a symbolic figure she personifies occult science waiting for the initiate on the threshold of the sanctuary of Isis in order to communicate nature's secrets to him. The Solar Cross (which is analogous with the Indian Lingam) denotes the fertilisation of matter by spirit. As the stamp of infinity, it also expresses the fact that knowledge proceeds from God, and is, like its source, without bounds. The veil descending from beneath the tiara and falling over the face signifies that truth stays well out of sight of profane curiosity. The book half-hidden beneath the cloak signifies that mysteries reveal themselves only in solitude, to the wise man who reflects in silence, and in full, calm possession of himself…

Remember child of Earth, that the mind finds enlightenment by seeking God with the eyes of the will. God said, "Let there be Light," and light inundated space. Man should say, "Let truth show itself and let good come to me!" And if man possesses a healthy will, he will see the light of truth shine, and with its guidance he will attain all the good he aspires to. If Arcanum II appears in your horoscope, knock resolutely on the door of the future and it will be opened to you. But study long and carefully the path you are to embark upon. Turn your face towards the Sun of Justice and the knowledge of what is true will be granted to you. Keep quiet about your purpose in order to avoid exposing it to human contradictions.

2

FRENCH: B

HEBREW: ג

SANSKRIT: ब

EGYPTIAN: 4 🕯

ARCHEOMETER OF SAINT-YVES: ⊖

THE HIGH PRIESTESS

DOUBLE LETTER

THE MOON

DIVINE SUBSTANCE
AIR
THE WOMAN—THE MOTHER

ETTEILLA 8. THE FEMALE QUERENT

Upright: This card represents the female querent. It represents the woman who is of most concern to the male querent, and it represents the female querent herself. Nature, repose, tranquillity, retreat, secluded life, solitude, peace and quiet of old age. Temple of ardour, silence, tenacity.

Reversed: Imitation, Garden of Eden, effervescence, seething, fermentation, ferment, leaven, acidity.

ISIS-URAMI, AND SYMBOLISES ACTION, WHICH IS A MANIFESTATION OF WILL COMBINED WITH KNOWLEDGE

In the divine world, G = 3 expresses the supreme power balanced by the eternally active intellect and by absolute wisdom. In the *intellectual world* it represents the universal fecundity of the supreme Being, and in the physical world, the work of nature, the germination of those acts which will be born of the Will.

Arcanum III is represented by a woman surrounded by the light of the sun. She is crowned by twelve stars and her feet rest on the moon. She is the personification of universal fecundity. The sun is the symbol of creative power. The crown of stars symbolises the 12 houses or stations of the zodiac through which the sun travels each year. The woman is celestial Isis or Nature. She carries a sceptre surmounted by a globe. This symbolises her perpetual action on things born and unborn. Her other hand bears an eagle, symbol of the heights to which spirit may soar. The moon beneath her feet signifies the lowliness of matter and its domination by the Spirit.

Remember, child of Earth, that to affirm what is true and to want what is just is already tantamount to creating those things. To affirm and to want the opposite is to devote oneself to destruction. If Arcanum III appears among the prophetic signs of your horoscope, then hope for success in your enterprises, provided you know how to combine activity, which is potentially fruitful, with the rectitude of mind that will make your labours bear fruit.

Etteilla 6. Night

Upright: In its natural position this card means situs, night, darkness, obscurity, light deprivation, nocturnal, mystery, secret, mask, hidden, unknown, clandestine, occult. Veil, emblem, figure, image, parabola, allegory, mystical fire, occult science. Secret manoeuvres, devious moves, clandestine actions. Blindness, to muddle or confuse, to cover, to envelop, difficulty, doubt, ignorance.

Reversed: Day, daylight, light, brightness, splendour, illumination, manifestation, evidence, truth. Clear, visible, luminous, to bring into being, to bring to light, publish, to open out or hatch. To pierce, to make a way for oneself, clearing or clarification, to acquire knowledge. Expedient, facility. Opening, window, empty or void, zodiac.

THE SEVENTY-EIGHT TAROT CARDS

FRENCH

HEBREW

SANSKRIT

EGYPTIAN

ARCHEOMETER OF SAINT-YVES

THE EMPRESS

DOUBLE LETTER

VENUS

DIVINE NATURE
WATER–THE MERCURY OF THE SAGES
GENERATION

CUBIC STONE, AND SYMBOLISES THE REALISATION OF HUMAN ACTS, THE WORK ACHIEVED

In the divine world, D = 4 expresses, the perpetual and hierarchical realisation of the virtualities contained in the absolute Being. In the *intellectual world*, it expresses the realisation of the ideas of the contingent Being through the fourfold work of the mind, namely, affirmation, negation, discussion, solution. In the physical world, it represents the realisation of actions guided by the knowledge of truth, love of justice, strength of will and the work of the [bodily] organs.

Arcanum IV is represented by a man wearing a helmet with a crown on top. He is seated on a cubical stone. In his right hand he has a sceptre. His right leg is bent and rests on the other in the shape of a cross. The cubical stone, the image of the perfect solid, denotes human labour accomplished. The crowned helmet symbolises strength that has won power. The man is a dominant figure. He bears the sceptre of Isis, and the stone which serves as his throne signifies the subjugation of matter. The cross formed by the position of his legs symbolises the four elements and the expansion of human power in all directions.

Remember, child of Earth, that nothing can resist a firm will which has the knowledge of truth and justice as its lever. Struggling to achieve the latter is more than a right, it is a duty. The man who wins this fight does no more than accomplish his mission here on earth. He who succumbs acquires immortality through devotion. If Arcanum IV appears in your horoscope, it means that the realisation of your hopes depends on a being more powerful than yourself. Seek them out and they will lend you their support.

Etteilla 7. Support

Upright: This card means backing, mainstay, support, buttress, column, base, foundation, basis. Principle, reason, cause, subject, fixity. Assurance, persuasion, conviction, safety, security, confidence, certainty. Aid, help, assistance, protection. Relief or comfort, consolation.

Reversed: Protection, influence, benevolence, beneficence, charity, humanity, goodness, commiseration, pity, compassion, credit. Authorisation.

THE SEVENTY-EIGHT TAROT CARDS

+4 □

FRENCH: D

HEBREW: ז

SANSKRIT: ट

EGYPTIAN

ARCHEOMETER OF SAINT-YVES: 2

JUPITER: ♃

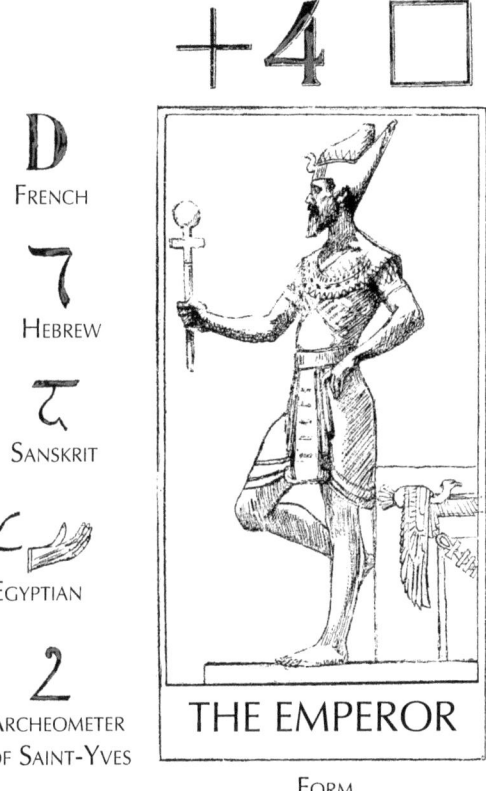

THE EMPEROR

FORM
FIRE "THE PHILOSOPHICAL CROSS"
AUTHORITY
PROTECTION

MASTER OF THE ARCANA, AND SYMBOLISES THE INSPIRATION THAT MAN GETS FROM THE OCCULT POWERS

In the divine world, E = 5 expresses the Universal Law, which governs the infinite manifestations of the Being within the unity of substance. In the *intellectual world*, it represents religion, the relationship of the absolute being to the relative being and of the infinite to the finite. In the physical world, it expresses inspiration, the testing of man through freedom of action within the closed circle of the universal law.

Arcanum V is represented by the image of the Hierophant (Master of the Sacred Mysteries). This prince of occult doctrine is seated between the two columns of the sanctuary. He is leaning on a cross with three horizontals. He is making the sign of silence across his breast with the index finger of his right hand. Two men are prostrate at his feet, one dressed in red the other in black. The Hierophant represents the spirit of good influence on the mind and the conscience. His gesture invites you to meditate and to listen to the voice of the heavens, silencing the passions and the instincts of the flesh. The column on his right symbolises divine law, the one on the left indicates freedom to obey or disobey. The cross with three horizontals is the emblem of God penetrating the three worlds in order to produce in them all manifestations of universal life. The two men prostrate men, one in red the other in black, represent the spirits of Light and of Darkness, both of whom obey the Master of the Arcana.

Remember, child of Earth, that before saying of a man that he is happy or unhappy, you must know to what use he puts his will. For all men create their lives in the image of their works. The spirit of good is on your right, the spirit of evil is on your left. Only your conscience hears their voices. Meditate, and it will answer you.

Etteilla 13. Marriage

Upright: From the point of view of spiritual healing this card means, marriage, union, junction, assembly, link, connection or tie, chain, slavery or bondage, discomfort or difficulty, captivity, servitude.

Reversed: Society, contacts, alloy, mixture, blending. Peace, concord, agreement, harmony, good terms.

E FRENCH

ה HEBREW

ऐ SANSKRIT

Ụ Ụ EGYPTIAN

♈ ARCHEOMETER OF SAINT-YVES

THE HIEROPHANT

♈ ARIES
20ᵀᴴ MARCH

UNIVERSAL MAGNETISM (SCIENCE OF GOOD AND EVIL)
QUINTESSENCE
RELIGION

TWO PATHS, AND SYMBOLISES THE TEST EVERY WILL IS SUBJECTED TO IN THE PRESENCE OF GOOD AND EVIL

In the divine world, U or V = 6 expresses the knowledge of good and evil. In the *intellectual world*, it expresses the balance between necessity and liberty. In the physical world, it expresses the antagonism of natural forces, the chain of cause and effect.

Arcanum VI is represented by a man standing motionless at a crossroads staring at the ground, his arms crossed upon his chest. On either side of him stands a woman, each with one hand placed on his shoulder, pointing out to him one of the two roads. The woman on his right has a gold band around her forehead. She personifies virtue. The one on the left wears a purple crown. She represents the temptations of vice. Above and behind this group, the spirit of justice, surrounded by an aura of dazzling light, is seen drawing his bow, directing the arrow of punishment at Vice. The whole scene expresses the struggle between the passions and the conscience.

Remember, child of Earth, that to the ordinary man, vice is more attractive than virtue. If Arcanum VI appears in your horoscope, take care to stick to your resolutions. Obstacles bar your path towards happiness; conflicting possibilities hover all around you. Your will wavers between opposing sides. In all things indecision is more fatal than making a wrong choice. Advance or retreat, but do not hesitate. Remember that a chain of flowers is more difficult to break than a chain of iron.

Etteilla 1. The Male Querent

Upright: It means God, the Supreme Being, the Central Spirit, Chaos. Meditation, reflection, concentration.
Reversed: The Universe. The physical man or the male. The querent.

THE SEVENTY-EIGHT TAROT CARDS

French

Hebrew

Sanskrit

Egyptian

Archeometer
of Saint-Yves

THE LOVER

Taurus
20th April

Creation
The Universal God
Liberty

CHARIOT OF OSIRIS, AND SYMBOLISES VICTORY, THAT IS TO SAY THE CHARIOT OF GOOD, WHICH IS THE FRUIT OF TRUTH AND JUSTICE

In the divine world, $Z = 7$ expresses the Septenary, the dominion of spirit over nature. In the *intellectual world*, it represents the priesthood and the empire. In the physical world, it represents the submission of the elements and the forces of matter to the intelligence and work of mankind.

Arcanum VII is represented by a square war-chariot surmounted by a starry canopy supported by four columns. An armed conqueror advances in the chariot, bearing a sceptre and a broadsword. He wears a crown consisting of a gold band decorated with three gold pentagrams or five-pointed stars. The square chariot symbolises work accomplished by the will in overcoming all obstacles. The four columns supporting the starry canopy represent the four elements tamed by the master of the sceptre and the sword. On the square representing the front of the chariot is a picture of a sphere supported by two outstretched wings, symbolising the boundless exaltation of human power in the infinity of space and time. The crown of gold on the conqueror's head denotes the possession of intellectual illumination which gives light to all the arcana of Fortune. The three stars decorating the crown symbolise power balanced by intellect and wisdom. The breast-plate is engraved with three squares, denoting rectitude of judgment, will and action as provided by the power symbolised by the breast-plate. The raised sword is a sign of victory. The sceptre surmounted by a triangle, symbol of the spirit, a square, symbol of matter and a circle, symbol of eternity, signifies the perpetual dominion of the mind over the forces of nature. Two sphinxes, one white, the other black, are harnessed to the chariot. One symbolises good, the other evil - the former won and the latter conquered - both now the servants of the Magus who has triumphed over his ordeals.

Remember child of Earth, that the empire of the world belongs to those who possess sovereignty of mind, that is to say, the light which illuminates the mysteries of life. By overcoming your obstacles you will crush your enemies, and all your wishes will be realised, if you go towards the future with courage reinforced by the knowledge that you are in the right.

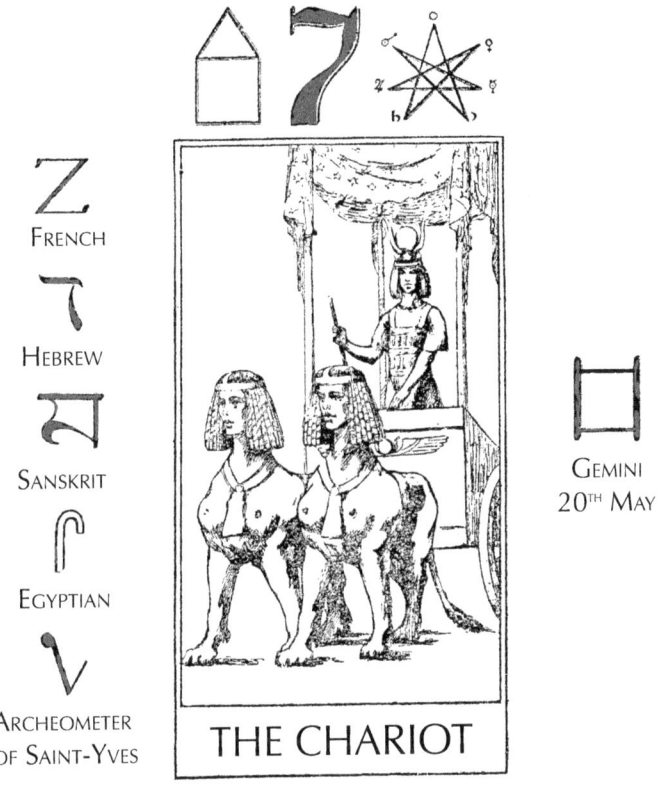

FRENCH

HEBREW

SANSKRIT

EGYPTIAN

ARCHEOMETER
OF SAINT-YVES

GEMINI
20ᵀᴴ MAY

THE CHARIOT

SPIRIT & FORM
VICTORY & TRIUMPH
PROPRIETY

ETTEILLA 21. DISAGREEMENT

Upright: From the point of view of spiritual healing this card means war, disagreement, dispute, noise, trouble, unrest, agitation, battle, struggle, combat. Arrogance, pride, vanity, false glory, pomp, ostentation, audacity, temerity. Violence, disorder, anger, insult, presumption, vengeance.

Reversed: Noise, uproar or scandal, quarrel, dispute, contestation, litigation, bother or interference, discussions.

THÉMIS, AND SYMBOLISES BALANCE, BY ANALOGY WITH THE BALANCE THAT IS THE ATTRIBUTE OF JUSTICE

In the divine world, H = 8 expresses absolute Justice. In the *intellectual world*, it expresses attraction and repulsion. In the physical world, it represents the relative, fallible and narrow-minded justice arising from mankind.

Arcanum VIII is represented by a woman seated on a throne and wearing a crown armed with spear-points. In her right hand is a broadsword, in her left hand a pair of scales. This is the ancient symbol of Justice weighing the deeds of men in the balance, with the sword of expiation as a counter-weight opposing evil. Justice, which issues forth from God, is the stabilising reaction, restoring order, i.e. the balance between rights and duty. The sword is here a sign of protection for the good and a threat to the wicked. The eyes of Justice are blindfold to show that she weighs things up and strikes without taking into account the conventional differences men establish among themselves.

Remember, child of Earth, that to be victorious and to overcome your obstacles is only part of the human task. In order to accomplish it fully you must establish a balance between the forces you set in motion. Every action produces a reaction, and the Will must foresee the impact of contrary forces in time to temper and check it! All futures hang in the balance between good and evil. The mind that cannot achieve balance resembles a sun in eclipse.

ETTEILLA 9. JUSTICE

Upright: From the point of view of spiritual healing this card means Justice, equity, probity, honesty, rectitude, reason. Justice, execution. Thoth or the book of Thoth.

Reversed: The legist. Legislation, legislator. Laws, code, statutes precepts, natural law, common law, public law, civil law, war legislation, the legist is governed directly by this hieroglyph.

THE SEVENTY-EIGHT TAROT CARDS 25

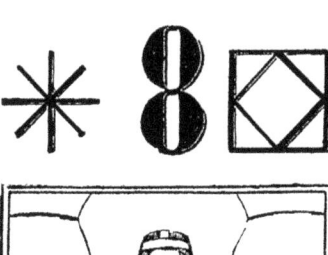

FRENCH

HEBREW

SANSKRIT

EGYPTIAN

ARCHEOMETER
OF SAINT-YVES

CANCER
20ᵀᴴ JUNE

JUSTICE

UNIVERSAL EQUILIBRIUM
DISTRIBUTION
JUSTICE

VEILED LAMP, AND SYMBOLISES PRUDENCE, WHICH MAINTAINS THE BALANCE

In the divine world, TH = 9 expresses absolute wisdom. In the *intellectual world*, it expresses prudence, the governor of the will, and in the physical world, circumspection, which guides actions.

Arcanum 9 is represented by an old man walking along leaning on a stick. In front of him he holds a lighted lantern, which is half hidden by his cloak. He personifies experience gained during a lifetime's work. The lighted lantern denotes the light of the intellect, which should illuminate the past, the present and the future, whilst the cloak which half conceals it signifies discretion. The stick symbolises the support lent by prudence to the man who does not reveal his thinking.

Remember, child of Earth, that prudence is the armour of the wise. Circumspection enables them to pitfalls and dangers and be forewarned of treachery. Make this your guide in all your actions and in even the most minor things. Nothing lacks importance down here. A stone can activate the chariot in which the master of the world is riding. Remember that if Speech is silver, Silence is golden.

Etteilla 18. Traitor

Upright: From the point of view of spiritual healing this card means, betrayal, disguise, deceit, hypocrisy, a traitor, a cheat, corrupter, seducer. Ruse, fraud or trickery.

Reversed: Loner, hermit, hidden, dissimulated, disguised. Politics, end.

THE SEVENTY-EIGHT TAROT CARDS

FRENCH — T
HEBREW — ט
SANSKRIT
EGYPTIAN
ARCHEOMETER OF SAINT-YVES

THE LION
20ᵗʰ JULY

THE HERMIT

GUARDIAN PROTECTORS
INITIATION
PRUDENCE

SPHINX, AND SYMBOLISES THE GOOD OR BAD FORTUNE THAT GOES WITH ALL ASPECTS OF LIFE

In the divine world, I, J, Y = 10 expresses the active principle that animates all beings. In the *intellectual world*, it expresses the ruling authority. In the physical world, it expresses good or bad fortune.

Arcanum X is represented by a wheel on its axle suspended between two columns. On the right Hermanubis, the Spirit of Good, strives to climb to the top of the wheel. On the left Typhon, the Spirit of Evil, is cast down. The Sphinx is balanced on the top of this wheel holding a sword in its lion's paws. It personifies Destiny, ever ready to strike left or right, allowing the humblest to rise and casting down the haughtiest depending on the direction in which it turns the wheel.

Remember, child of Earth, that enablement is dependent upon will, and in order to will effectively you must dare, and in order to dare successfully you must be able to keep silent until the moment comes for action. In order to acquire the right to possess knowledge and power, you must apply will patiently and with tireless perseverance. And in order to reach the heights of life and stay there, you must first have learned to plumb the vastest depths without succumbing to dizziness.

Etteilla 20. Fortune

Upright: From the point of view of spiritual healing this card means good luck, happiness, improvement, bonus, prosperity, assets, riches, benefits. Grace, favours. Fate, destiny, adventures, good fortune.

Reversed: Development, expansion, abundance, extras. Growth, vegetation, production.

THE SEVENTY-EIGHT TAROT CARDS

I Y
FRENCH

ל
HEBREW

प
SANSKRIT

EGYPTIAN

ARCHEOMETER
OF SAINT-YVES

10

THE WHEEL OF FORTUNE

THE KINGDOM OF GOD
ORDER
FORTUNE

♍
VIRGO
20ᵀᴴ AUGUST

TAMED LION, AND SYMBOLISES THE FORCE THAT ALL MEN ARE CALLED UPON TO CONQUER THROUGH DEVELOPING THEIR INTELLECTUAL AND MORAL FACULTIES

In the divine world, C, K = 20 expresses the principle of all strength: spiritual or material. In the *intellectual world* it represents moral strength and in the physical world bodily strength.

Arcanum XI is represented by the image of a young girl closing the jaws of a lion effortlessly with her bare hands. This is symbolic of the strength which is imparted by faith in oneself and by innocence in life.

Remember, child of Earth, that enablement depends on faith in your ability to accomplish what you set out to do. Proceed with faith; the obstacles are phantoms. In order to become strong, you must silence all weaknesses of heart. You must study duty since right is subject to it, and practise justice as if you loved it.

Etteilla 11. Strength

Upright: From the point of view of spiritual healing this card means strength, heroism, magnanimity, grandeur, courage. Power, might, empire, ascendant. Spiritual work, patience, resignation, Thoth or the book of Thoth.

Reversed: Sovereign, kingdom, State, republic, government, administration, reign, tyranny, sovereignty, supreme power, arbitrary power, people, nation, weakness, defectiveness, discord.

THE SEVENTY-EIGHT TAROT CARDS 31

FRENCH

HEBREW

SANSKRIT

ᘓ
EGYPTIAN

ARCHEOMETER
OF SAINT-YVES

STRENGTH

MARS

DIVINE STRENGTH
MORAL STRENGTH
HUMAN STRENGTH

SACRIFICE, AND SYMBOLISES VIOLENT DEATH

In the divine world, L = 30 expresses the revelation of the law. In the *intellectual world*, it expresses the teaching of duty. In the physical world it expresses sacrifice.

Arcanum XII is represented by a man hung by one foot from a gallows. The gallows pole is laid across two trees, each with six branches lopped from the trunk. The man's hands are tied behind his back, and the crook of the arms forms the base of an inverted triangle, the apex of this being his head. This symbolises violent death suffered as a result of a tragic accident, or in expiation of a crime, or else accepted in a spirit of heroic devotion to truth and justice. The twelve lopped branches represent the extinction of life, the destruction of the twelve houses of the Horoscope. The reversed triangle symbolises a catastrophe.

Remember, child of Earth, that devotion is a divine law from which no-one is exempt. But expect little other than ingratitude from men. Let your heart be ready to give account to the Eternal at all times, for if Arcanum XII appears in your horoscope, violent death will set traps for you along the way. But if the world makes an attempt on your earthly life, do not die without accepting God's judgement upon you with resignation and without pardoning even your cruellest enemies, for whoever fails to forgive while on earth will be condemned to eternal solitude in the life beyond.

Etteilla 12. Prudence

Upright: From the point of view of spiritual healing this card means prudence, reserve, wisdom, circumspection, restraint, discernment, foresight, provision. Premonition, prognosis, prophet. Thoth or the book of Thoth.

Reversed: Nation, legislator, body politic, population, generation.

12

FRENCH
L

HEBREW
ל

SANSKRIT
ह

EGYPTIAN
K

ARCHEOMETER
OF SAINT-YVES
ʒ

LIBRA
20ᵀᴴ SEPTEMBER

THE HANGED MAN

ACCOMPLISHMENT/COMPLETION
MORAL SACRIFICE
PHYSICAL SACRIFICE

SICKLE, AND SYMBOLISES MAN'S TRANSFORMATION, THAT IS TO SAY HIS PASSAGE INTO THE FUTURE LIFE THROUGH NATURAL DEATH

In the divine world, M = 40 expresses the perpetual movement of creation, destruction and renewal. In the *intellectual world*, it expresses the ascent of the spirit into the divine spheres. In the physical world it expresses death, that is to say, the transformation of human nature once it reaches the end of its final bodily phase.

Arcanum XIII is represented by a skeleton reaping heads in a meadow, while men's hands and feet lie on the ground all around as the scythe pursues its task. This is symbolic of the perpetual destruction and rebirth of all forms of being within the domain of Time.

Remember, child of Earth, that earthly things last only for a brief time, and the loftiest of powers are cut down like the grass in the fields. Your visible organs will decay sooner than you expect. But do not fear this, for death is merely birth into another life. The universe ceaselessly reabsorbs all that leaves its breast and has not been spiritualised. But the freeing of material instincts through the soul's free and voluntary adherence to the laws of universal movement constitutes in us the creation of a second man, the celestial man, and this marks the beginning of our immortality.

Etteilla 17. Mortality

Upright: From the point of view of spiritual healing this card means death, mortality, annihilation or ruin, destruction. End, deterioration, debasement or adulteration, rot, corruption, putrefaction.

Reversed: Inertia, sleep, lethargy, petrification. Annihilation or ruin, somnambulism.

THE SEVENTY-EIGHT TAROT CARDS 35

M
FRENCH

HEBREW

SANSKRIT

EGYPTIAN

ARCHEOMETER
OF SAINT-YVES

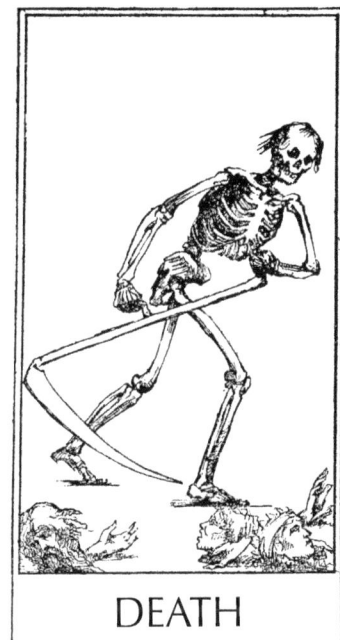

MOTHER LETTER

DEATH

IMMORTALITY THROUGH CHANGE
DEATH AND REBIRTH
THE TRANSMUTATION OF FORCES

SOLAR SPIRIT, AND SYMBOLISES HUMAN INITIATIVE THROUGH COMBINED WILL, KNOWLEDGE AND ACTION

In the divine world, N = 50 expresses the perpetual movement of life. In the *intellectual world*, it expresses the combination of the ideas which create the moral life. In the physical world, it expresses the combination of the forces of nature.

Arcanum XIV is represented by the Spirit of the Sun holding two urns. He is pouring the vital sap of life from one into the other. This symbolises the combinations constantly being made in every realm of nature.

Child of Earth, take stock of your strength, not in order to shrink from the tasks you face, but in order to erode obstacles just as water falling drop by drop wears away even the hardest stone.

ETTEILLA 10. TEMPERANCE

Upright: From the point of view of spiritual healing this card means temperance, moderation, frugality, chastity, softening, thoughtfulness or solicitude, arrangement or compromise. Respect, consideration. Temperature, climate, Thoth or the book of Thoth.

Reversed: Minister, priest, clergy, church, religion, sect, the querent is under the influence of such powers.

14

N FRENCH		
ℶ HEBREW		♏
त SANSKRIT		SCORPIO 20ᵀᴴ OCTOBER
 EGYPTIAN		
◡ ARCHEOMETER OF SAINT-YVES		

TEMPERANCE

REVERSIBILITY
HARMONY OF MIXTURES
TEMPERANCE

TYPHON, AND SYMBOLISES FATE, WHICH STRIKES UNEXPECTEDLY

In the divine world, X = 60 expresses predestination. In the *intellectual world*, it expresses mystery and in the physical world, the unforeseen, fatality.

Arcanum XV is represented by Typhon, the spirit of catastrophes, rising out of a flaming abyss brandishing torches above the heads of two men chained at his feet. This is the image of fatality, which bursts into some lives like an erupting volcano, overwhelming the great and the small, the strong and the weak, the cleverest and the least clever, since disaster is a great leveller.

Whoever you may be, child of Earth, contemplate the ancient oaks that defied the lightning, but the lightning then struck them after having left them alone for more than a century. Cease to believe in your wisdom and your strength unless God has granted you permission to grasp the key to the mysteries of Fate.

Etteilla 14. Force Majeure

Upright: From the point of view of spiritual healing this card means force majeure, great movement, vehemence, extraordinary efforts, force or strength, extraordinary power, powers. Virtue, property or power, impetus or impulse. Flights of genius. Devastation or havoc, violence, physical work.

Reversed: Slightness, weakness, paltriness, failure.

15

French: स

Hebrew: ס

Sanskrit: श्र

Egyptian: ·

Archeometer of Saint-Yves

THE DEVIL

→ Sagittarius
20ᵀᴴ November

Destiny
The Magic Serpent (the magic agent)
Physical Life

TOWER STRUCK BY LIGHTNING, AND SYMBOLISES RUIN, IN ALL ITS VARIOUS ASPECTS

In the divine world, O = 70 expresses the punishment of pride. In the *intellectual world*, it expresses the downfall of the spirit who attempts to delve into the mysteries of God. In the physical world, it expresses reversals of fortune.

Arcanum XVI is represented by a tower struck by lightning, with a crowned and an uncrowned man being thrown down from the heights along with debris from the ruined battlements. This symbolises the material forces that can crush great and small, kings and subjects alike. It is also symbolic of rivalries, which only end in ruin for all concerned, of plans that come to nothing, of hopes that fade and of abortive enterprises, crushed ambitions and catastrophic deaths.

Remember, child of Earth, that all trials of misfortune accepted with resignation to the supreme will of the All-Powerful constitute progress for which you will be eternally rewarded. Suffering means working to free yourself from the bonds of material things, it means putting on the robes of immortality.

Etteilla 19. Distress

Upright: From the point of view of spiritual healing, in its natural position, this card means situs, misery or wretchedness, distress, destitution, poverty, shortage, need, necessity, calamity, adversity, misfortune, trouble, torment, pain, affliction, annoyance or inconvenience, penalty, correction, punishment. Rude awakening, disgrace, severity, rigidity, rigour.

Reversed: Imprisonment, detention, arrest, captivity, oppression, tyranny, subjection, subjugation.

THE SEVENTY-EIGHT TAROT CARDS   41

FRENCH

HEBREW

SANSKRIT

EGYPTIAN

ARCHEOMETER
OF SAINT-YVES

THE HOUSE OF GOD

CAPRICORN
20ᵀᴴ DECEMBER

DESTRUCTION THROUGH ANTAGONISM
DISRUPTION OF MATERIAL EQUILIBRIUM
RUIN CATASTROPHE

STAR OF THE MAGI, AND SYMBOLISES HOPE, WHICH LEADS TO SALVATION THROUGH FAITH

In the divine world, F, P = 80 expresses immortality. In the *intellectual world*, it expresses the inner light that illuminates the spirit. In the physical world, it expresses hope.

Arcanum XVII is represented by a bright star with eight rays surrounded by seven other stars above a naked girl pouring the waters of universal life over the barren earth as they flow from two goblets, one gold, the other silver. Beside her is a butterfly about to alight on a rose. The girl symbolises hope, which scatters its dew on even our bleakest days. Her nakedness signifies that hope remains with us when we have been stripped of everything. The bright eight-pointed star above her symbolises the apocalypse of fates, sealed by seven seals constituting the seven planets as represented by the other seven stars. The butterfly is a symbol of resurrection beyond the grave.

Remember, child of Earth, that hope is the sister of faith. Strip away your passions and your errors and study the mysteries of true knowledge, and the key to them will be yours. A ray of the divine light will then shine out from the occult sanctuary and dispel the darkness of the future, showing you the path to happiness. Never crush the flowers of hope no matter what happens in your life. That way you will harvest the fruits of faith.

Etteilla 4. Dispossession

Upright: This card means dispossession, deprivation, destitution, abandonment, analysis, essence/extract, balancing the books, sorting, separation, depredation/misappropriation/embezzlement, despoilment, theft, losses, being deprived of help.

Reversed: Air, wind, storm, atmosphere, climate, drought, sky, stars. Birds, subtle, volatile, tone. Manner, affectation, trick, appearance or bearing, physiognomy, resemblance. Groundless scandal. Arrogance, hauteur, importance, song, music, melody.

Ph.
FRENCH

HEBREW

SANSKRIT

EGYPTIAN

ARCHEOMETER
OF SAINT-YVES

THE STAR

MERCURY

NATURAL DIVINE FORCES
NATURE
FECUNDITY

TWILIGHT, AND SYMBOLISES THE DECEPTIONS, WHICH TEACH US OUR WEAKNESS

In the divine world, TS = 90 expresses the depths of infinity. In the *intellectual world*, it expresses the darkness that envelops the spirit when it submits to the influence of the instincts. In the physical world, it expresses deceit and hidden enemies.

Arcanum XVIII is represented by a field lit by a half-clouded moon in a pale twilight sky. A tower stands on either side of a path which disappears over the bare horizon. In front of one of the two towers is a crouching dog, in front of the other is a wolf howling at the moon. Between them is a crab. The towers symbolise a false sense of security which fails to foresee hidden perils.

Remember, child of Earth, that whoever dares to confront the unknown is heading for ruin. Hostile spirits, symbolised by the wolf, wait in ambush, servile spirits, symbolised by the dog, conceal their treachery beneath base flattery, and idle spirits, symbolised by the crab, will pass by without the slightest concern for the disaster. Observe, listen—and learn to keep silent.

Etteilla 3. Proposal

Upright: This card means proposal, discussion, conversation, discourse, interview, talking, gossiping, chatting. Malicious gossip, slander, order/decree, resolution. Moon.

Reversed: Flowing water, dew, rain, sea, river, tributary, spring, torrent, fountain, stream, lake, marshland, stagnant pool, sheet of water/groundwater, pond. Humidity, impregnated vapour, smoke, mercury, chaotic and philosophical water. Emanation, frost, snow, exhalation, evaporation. Instability, inconstancy, silence. Murmur. Patient.

THE SEVENTY-EIGHT TAROT CARDS

18

THE MOON

T s
FRENCH

HEBREW
SANSKRIT

ㄴ
EGYPTIAN

ϱ
ARCHEOMETER
OF SAINT-YVES

AQUARIUS
20ᵀᴴ JANUARY

HIERARCHICAL DISTRIBUTION OF LIGHT
OCCULT FORCES
HIDDEN ENEMIES

SHINING LIGHT AND SYMBOLISES EARTHLY HAPPINESS

In the divine world, Q = 100 expresses High Heaven. In the *intellectual world*, it expresses sacred truth and, in the physical world, peaceful well-being.

Arcanum XIX is represented by a radiant sun shining on the figures of two small children, images of innocence, holding hands in the middle of a circle dotted with flowers. This symbolises the promise of happiness brought about by a simple life and moderation in one's desires.

Remember, child of Earth, that the light of mystery is a formidable force, which nature places at the service of the will. It illuminates those who know how to handle it, but it strikes down those who are ignorant of its power or who abuse it.

Etteilla 2. Enlightenment

Upright: This card means enlightenment, light, explanation. Clarity or limpidity, glory, heaven and earth. – Philosophical sulphur.

Reversed: Fire. Warmth, glow. Blaze. Flame, passions. Meteors, lightning, thunder. Internal, external and philosophical fire.

THE SEVENTY-EIGHT TAROT CARDS

19

K
FRENCH

ק
HEBREW

क
SANSKRIT

ʕ◠
EGYPTIAN

X
ARCHEOMETER
OF SAINT-YVES

PISCES
20ᵀᴴ FEBRUARY

THE SUN

THE TRUE LIGHT
PHILOSOPHICAL GOLD
FECUND TRUTH

AWAKENING OF THE DEAD, AND SYMBOLISES THE RENEWAL THAT TURNS GOOD INTO EVIL OR EVIL INTO GOOD IN THE SERIES OF TRIALS THAT ALL PATHWAYS THROUGH LIFE IMPOSE UPON US

R = 200 represents the passage from life on earth to the future life. A Spirit is playing a bugle over a half-open grave. A man, a woman and a child, symbolising the human trinity, are seen rising from the grave. This signifies the change which marks the end of all things, good as well as evil.

Remember, child of Earth, that fortune is fickle, even when it appears at its most stable. The soul's ascent is the fruit of its successive trials. Hope in times of suffering, but be wary in times of prosperity. Do not be lulled into laziness or forgetfulness. At some point, unknown to you, the wheel of fortune will turn, and you will be elevated or cast down by the Sphinx.

Etteilla 16. Judgement

Upright: From the point of view of spiritual healing this card means judgement, devotion, intelligence, concept or understanding, reason, good sense. Reasoning, comparison. View, suspicion, thought. Opinion, feeling, dissolution.

Reversed: Arrest, decree, deliberation, decision, weak mind, pusillanimity. Simplicity.

20

French: R

Hebrew: ר

Sanskrit: र

Egyptian: /

Archeometer of Saint-Yves

JUDGEMENT

Saturn: ♄

Protection by Divided Forces
Moral Rebirth
Change of Circumstances

CROCODILE, AND SYMBOLISES THE EXPIATION OF VOLUNTARY ERRORS OR FAULTS

S = 300 represents the punishment that ensues from each error. Here you see a blind man carrying a full beggar's bag about to bump into a broken obelisk, upon which a crocodile waits with open jaws. The blind man is symbolic of the person who has become a slave to material things. His bag is filled with his errors and faults. The broken obelisk represents the downfall of his deeds, and the crocodile is a symbol of implacable fate and inevitable expiation.

Etteilla 78. Folly

Upright: From the point of view of spiritual healing, in its natural position, this card means: madness, lunacy or folly, dementia, extravagance, unreasonableness, distraction, drunkenness, delirium, frenzy, abnormality or unsoundness, fury, transport, outburst or outpouring. Enthusiasm. Blindness or blinkered state, ignorance. Fool or madman, absurd, irrational, innocent, simple, simple-minded or inane.

Reversed: Idiocy, ineptitude, carefreeness, casualness or happy-go-lucky state of mind, nonsense, imprudence, negligence, absence, distraction. Apathy, fainting, exhaustion or annihilation, sleep, nothingness or emptiness, uselessness or nullity, empty or void, nothing. Vain.

THE SEVENTY-EIGHT TAROT CARDS 51

0

Sh
FRENCH

שׁ
HEBREW

श
SANSKRIT

△
EGYPTIAN

ARCHEOMETER
OF SAINT-YVES

MOTHER LETTER

THE FOOL

BREAK IN DIVINE COMMUNICATIONS
MORAL BLINDNESS
MATTER

CROWN OF THE MAGI, AND SYMBOLISES THE REWARD GIVEN TO ALL MEN WHO FULFIL THEIR MISSION ON EARTH WHILE MIRRORING SOME OF THE FEATURES OF THE IMAGE OF GOD

This supreme Arcanum of mageship is represented by a garland of gold roses surrounding a star, and placed within a circle around which are the heads of four equidistant figures: a man, a bull, a lion and an eagle. This is the emblem with which the magus decorates himself when he has reached the highest degree of initiation and has therefore acquired powers, the ascensional levels of which are limited only by his own intelligence and wisdom.

Remember, child of Earth, that world dominion belongs to the realm of Light, and the realm of Light is the throne reserved by God for the sanctified will. To the magus, happiness is the fruit of the knowledge of good and evil. But God only allows this fruit to be plucked by the man who is sufficiently master of himself to approach it without coveting it.

ETTEILLA 5. JOURNEY

Upright: This card means journey, route or road, walk or march, approach, displacement, peregrination, visit, race, foray, emigration, migration, Judge. Retreat. Rotation, circulation or traffic. Disorientate, disconcert.

Reversed: Earth, matter, mud, vase, silt. Raw material, sulphur and mercury, salt of the sages, cold, thick. Female gnome, world, terrestrial globe, State, kingdom, empire. Terrain, territory, possessions, rural goods. Aspect, permanence, fixity, stagnation. Inertia. Animals, brute. Sepulchre, tomb. Ash, powder, dust. Matter, philosophical salt.

21

Th
FRENCH

ת
HEBREW

SANSKRIT

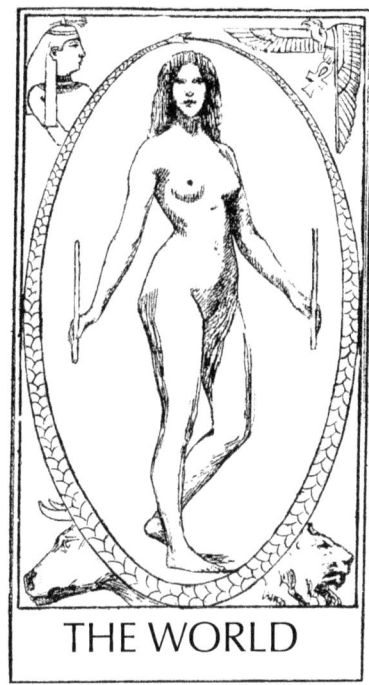

THE WORLD

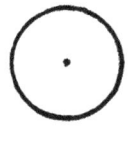
THE SUN

ARCHEOMETER
OF SAINT-YVES

THE ABSOLUTE
REALISATION OF THE GREAT WORK
CERTAIN TRIUMPH

By linking one to the other, and subsequently the 22 meanings arising from these symbols, the resulting whole forms a synthesis of magism, as follows:

The human Will (I), enlightened by Knowledge (II) and manifested in Action (III), created by the Realisation (IV) of a power which one uses or abuses depending on one's good or bad Inspiration (V) within the circle traced by the laws of the universal order.

After having overcome the Trial (VI) imposed upon it by divine wisdom, through its own Victory (VII) it comes into possession of the work it has created, and finding its Balance (VIII) on the axis of Prudence (IX), it then dominates the vacillations of Fortune (X).—The Strength (XI) of man, sanctified by Sacrifice (XII), which amounts to the voluntary offering up of oneself on the altar of devotion or expiation. The triumph of Death, and its divine Transformation (XIII), elevates it beyond the grave to the tranquil areas of infinite progress, as opposed to the reality of an immortal Initiative (XIV), and to the eternal lie of Fate (XV).

The passage of time is measured in ruins, but beyond each Ruin (XVI), we see the dawn of Hope (XVII) reappear or the twilight of Deceptions (XVIII). Man constantly aspires to that which eludes him, and the sun of happiness only arises for him beyond the grave and after the Renewal (XX) of his being through the death that opens up a higher sphere of will, intelligence and action.—All will that allows itself to be governed by bodily instincts is a renunciation of freedom, and must then devote itself to the Expiation (0) of its error or fault.—By contrast, the will that unites with God in order to manifest truth and bring about justice becomes a participant in this lifetime in divine power over beings and things.

THE MINOR ARCANA

Here is the arrangement used for the minor arcana.

In the centre is the drawing reconstituted by Gabriel Goulinat on the basis of Egyptian documents and the personal work of Eliphas Levi. The engravings at the bottom of each of the cards are reproductions of the secret talismans of Eliphas Levi.

The area around the central drawing is divided into four sections: top, bottom, right and left. The divinatory meanings according to Etteilla are shown at the top and bottom of each card: upright at the top, reversed at the bottom.

For details of the divinatory meanings we have included the work of Odoucet and Etteilla along side each card.

On the right [of each card] you find all the information about the exact time, and that is an extremely important innovation from a divinatory point of view. First of all there are the corresponding days of the month in ten day periods. Then there are the corresponding quarters of the moon, day by day, and lastly the corresponding hours of each day.

Thus the Ace of Wands corresponds to the period from 1st to 10th March in relation to the sun and the first day of the first quarter of the moon and to 6 a.m. in relation to the day. A few other correspondences are shown on the bottom right hand side.

On the left is the correspondence to the philosophical Tarot as determined by Eliphas Levi, this being the linking factor between *Divinatory Tarot* and my work on the *Tarot of the Bohemians*.

King of Wands

Upright: From the point of view of spiritual healing, in its natural position, this card means countryman, good and austere man, well-intentioned man, honest man. Conscience, probity. Agriculturist, labourer, farmer.

Reversed: Good and austere man. Indulgence, severity or austerity, tolerance, condescension.

22
By Etteilla

King of
Wands

Yod-Yod

The
Father

King of
Wands

Head Man

Man of
will and
Enterprise

Dark man

BB

KING OF WANDS

Queen of Wands

Upright: From the point of view of spiritual healing, in its natural position, this card means countrywoman, housewife, economy, honesty, civility. Gentleness, virtue. Honour, chastity.

Reversed: Good woman, goodness, excellence. Obliging, informal, helpful. Benefit, service, obligation.

23
By Etteilla

Yod-He

Wife of the Father

Queen of Wands

Woman of enterprise

Dark woman

BN

QUEENS OF WANDS

Knight of Wands

Upright: From the point of view of spiritual healing, in its natural position, this card means departure, displacement, distance or removal, absence, abandonment, change, flight, desertion, migration, emigration. Transposition, translation, transplantation, transmutation, evasion.

Reversed: Disunion, misunderstanding, rupture, dissent, division, part, separation, apportioning. Faction, party. Quarrel or feud, altercation. Cut, fracture, discontinuation, interruption.

24
By Etteilla

Yod-He

Powerful conqueror

Knight of Wands

Setting off (envoy to a chief)

Dark youth

BS

KNIGHT OF WANDS

Page of Wands

Upright: From the point of view of spiritual healing, in its natural position, this card means stranger or foreigner, unknown, extraordinary. Foreign or strange, unusual, unaccustomed, incredible, surprising, admirable, wonderful or marvellous, marvel or wonder, miracle. Episode, digression, anonymous.

Reversed: Announcement, instruction, notification, warning, admonition, anecdotes, chronicle, history or story, tales or legends, fables, notions, teaching.

25
By Etteilla

Yod-He

Slave of man

Page of Wands

Chief's envoy

Good stranger/foreigner

BL

PAGE OF WANDS

Ten of Wands

Upright: From the point of view of spiritual healing, in its natural position, this card means betrayal, perfidy, treachery, deception, ruse, surprise, disguise, deceit, hypocrisy, prevarication, duplicity, disloyalty, dark deeds, falseness, conspiracy. Fraud.

Reversed: Obstacle, eagerness or enthusiasm. Bar, obstacle, setbacks, difficulties, trouble, work. Inconvenience or discomfort, abjection, quibbling or petty squabbling, complaint, pitfall, hurdle, retrenchment or entrenchment, redoubt, fortification.

26
By Etteilla

Betrayal

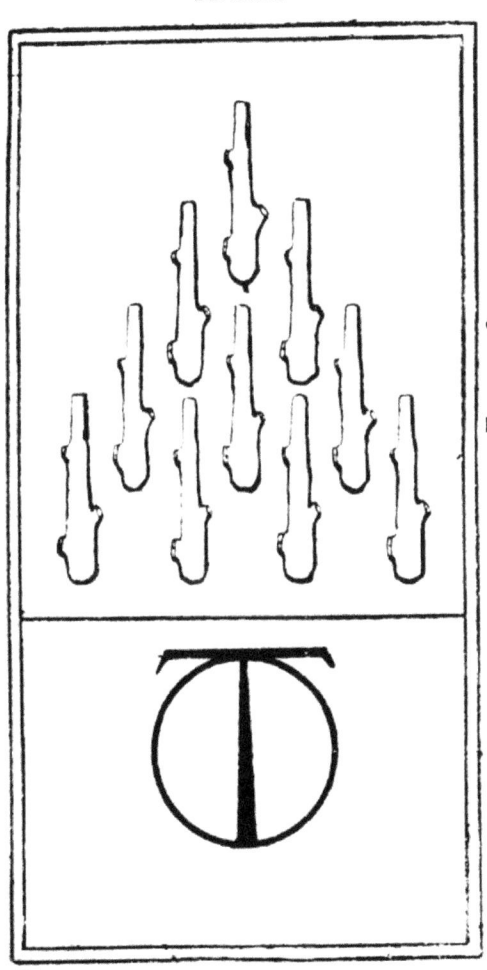

June 1st

or uncertain date May-June

First quarter to Full Moon

11 a.m. to midday

Young woman 20 years old

BLNS

Bars
Ten of Wands

Nine of Wands

Upright: From the point of view of spiritual healing, in its natural position, this card means lateness, delay, distance or removal, delivery, return or postponement, suspension, extension, slowly, slowing down.

Reversed: Setback, obstacle, hitch, vexation, disadvantage, adversity, trouble, misfortune, sorrows, calamity.

THE SEVENTY-EIGHT TAROT CARDS 67

27
By Etteilla

Delay

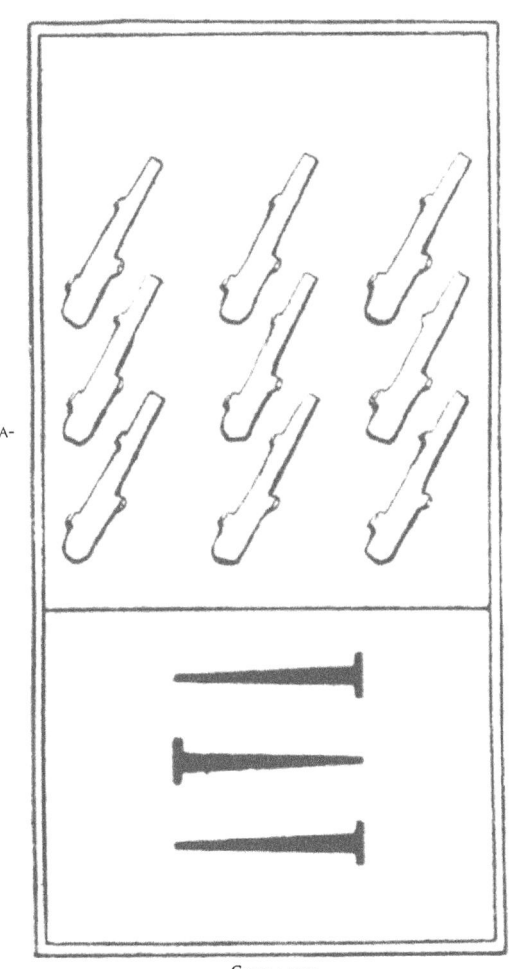

Consola-
tion

May 20ᵀᴴ
to 30ᵀᴴ

First
Quarter
= 6ᵀᴴ day
and 6ᵀᴴ
night

10 to 11
a.m.

Young
man from
16 to 18
years old

BLSN

Setbacks
Nine of Wands

Eight of Wands

Upright: From a healing point of view, in its natural position, this card means countryside, field, plain, agriculture, farming or crop growing, tilling or ploughing, real estate, building, farm, sharecropping farm, garden, orchard, meadow, wood, copse, shade, canopy or foliage, pleasure, entertainment, amusement, pastime, recreation, rejoicing, peace, calm, tranquillity, innocence, rustic life, forest, dell, mountain, battlefield.

Reversed: Domestic quarrel, examination, reasoning, misunderstanding or discord, regrets, remorse, repentance, agitation within, indecisiveness, uncertainty, indecision inconceivable, incomprehensible, doubt, scruple, easily alarmed or jumpy.

28
By Etteilla

Day Trip to the Country

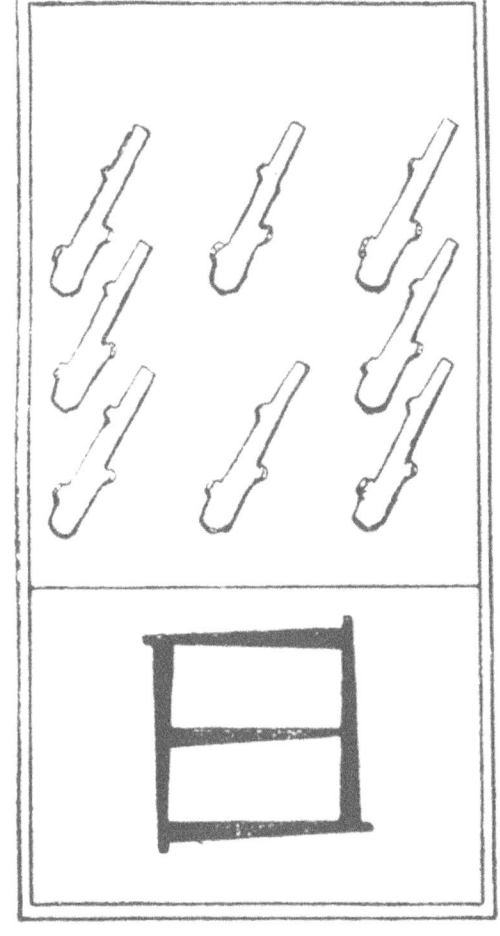

Providence

May 10th to 20th

First Quarter = 4th night

9.30 a.m.

Girl from 14 to 16 years old

BSNL

Internecine struggles
Eight of Wands

Seven of Wands

Upright: From the point of view of spiritual healing, in its natural position, this card means negotiation, interview or discussion, conference, colloquium, conversation, essay or speech, deliberation, resolution, decision, discussion. Speech, pronouncement, language, idiom, patois or dialect, negotiation, transaction, exchange, measure, commerce, traffic, correspondence. Talk, say, utter, confer, gossip, chat, divide, prattle, blab.

Reversed: Indecisiveness, uncertainty, indecision, perplexity, inconstancy, casualness or irresponsibility, variation, variety, diversity, to hesitate, hesitation. To wobble, to vacillate, versatility.

THE SEVENTY-EIGHT TAROT CARDS 71

29
BY ETTEILLA

GOSSIP

GRAND GOALS

MAY 1ST TO 10TH

FIRST QUARTER = 4TH DAY

9.30 A.M.

BOY FROM 12 TO 14 YEARS OLD

BSNL

INDECISION
SEVEN OF WANDS

Six of Wands

Upright: From the point of view of spiritual healing, in its natural position, this card means: domestic servant, manservant, valet, lackey, maidservant, mercenary, inferior, slave. Messenger, agent or broker, housekeeper or housekeeping.— Indoor part of the house, household, family, the whole household staff.

Reversed: Wait, hope, expectation, to rely or depend upon, to build upon, to trust, to make up one's mind. Confidence or reliance, foresight, precaution or providence. Fear, apprehension.

30
By Etteilla

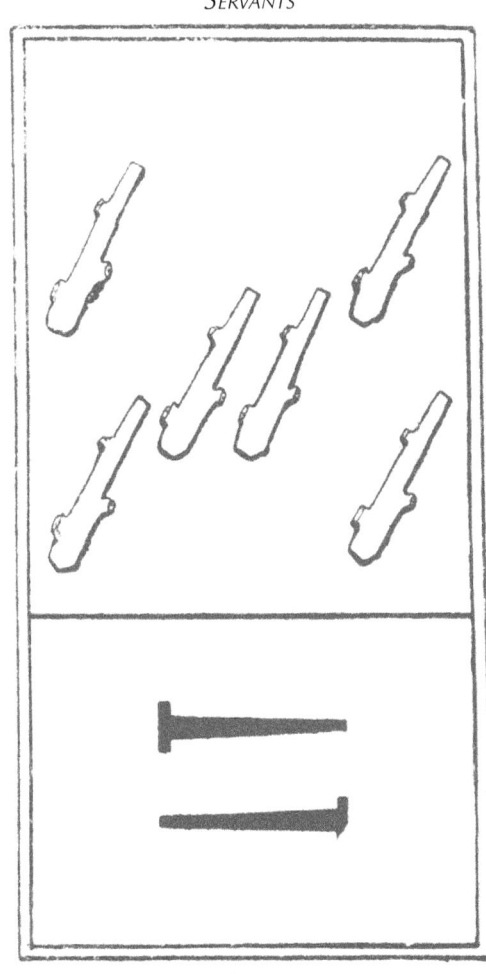

Servants

Divine consolation

April 20th to 30th

First Quarter = 3rd night

8.30a.m

Girl from 10 to 12 years old

BSLN

Waiting
Six of Wands

Five of Wands

Upright: From the point of view of spiritual healing, in its natural position, this card means gold, wealth, opulence, splendour, sumptuousness, display or showiness, luxury, abundance, property.—Physical, philosophical and moral sun.

Reversed: Trial, litigation disagreement, contention, contestations, disputes, proceedings, investigation, examination or lawsuit. Vexation, discussions, chicanery, quibbling, pestering or interference.—Contradiction, inconsistency or inconsequentiality.

THE SEVENTY-EIGHT TAROT CARDS

31
By Etteilla

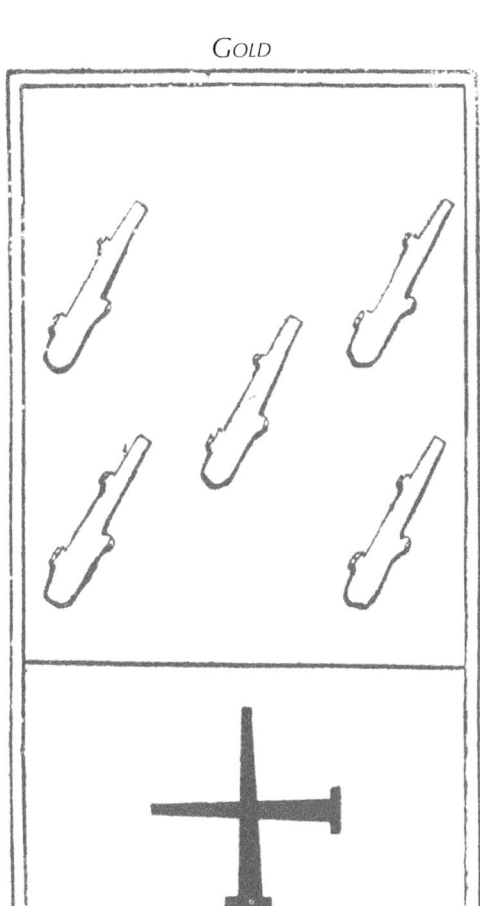

Gold

Object of worship

April 10th to 20th

First Quarter = 3rd day

8 a.m.

Boy child from 8 to 10 years old

BSLN

Trial
Five of Wands

Four of Wands

Upright: From the point of view of spiritual healing, in its natural position, this card means: company, association or partnership, liaison, federation, alliance, assembly, meeting, circle, community, gathering, multitude, crowd, throng or melee, troops, band, company, cohort, army. Convocation, accompaniment, blending or compounding, mixture, alloy, amalgam. - Contract, convention, pact, treaty.

Reversed: Prosperity, increase, growth, advancement, achievement, success, good fortune or well-being, flourishing, happiness. Beauty, embellishment.

32
By Etteilla

Company

WORD
MADE
FATHER

April 1ˢᵗ
to 10ᵀᴴ

First
Quarter =
2ᴺᴰ night

7.30 a.m.

Girls
from 8 to
10 years

BNLS

Flowering
Four of Wands

Three of Wands

Upright: From the point of view of spiritual healing, in its natural position, this card means: enterprise, to undertake, to begin. To usurp, to seize. Daring, boldness, audacity or impudence, temerity, recklessness, foolhardiness or rashness. Imprudence, enterprising, bold, foolhardy, rash or reckless, bold or impudent. Undertaken, embarrassed or confused. Disconcerted. Crippled or paralysed, effort, attempt, temptation.

Reversed: Pause in misfortune or sorrow, torment, pain or work. End, cessation, discontinuation, respite, rest, influence, intermediary, intermittence.

33
By Etteilla

Enterprise

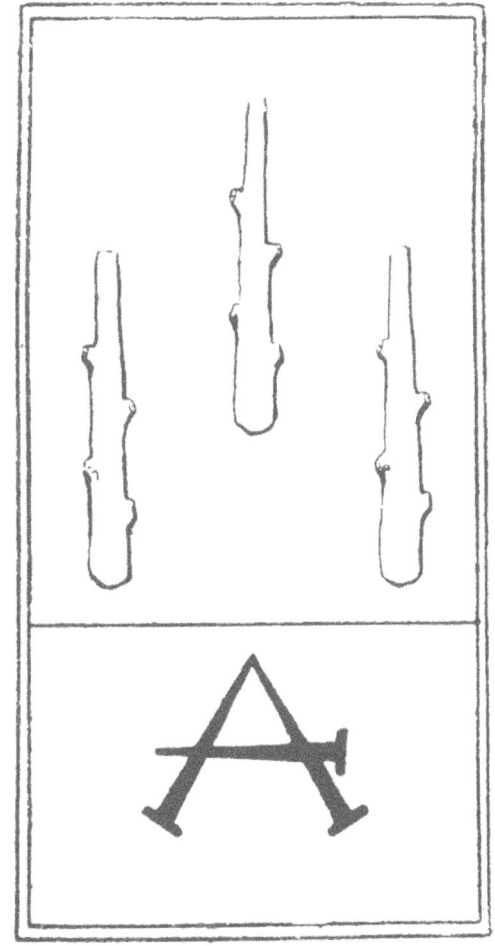

Divine hope

March 20th to 30th

First quarter = 2nd day

7 a.m

Male child from 4 to 6 years old

BNLS

Sorrow's end
Three of Wands

Two of Wands

Upright: From the point of view of spiritual healing, in its natural position, this card means: sorrow, sadness, melancholy, affliction, displeasure, pain, desolation, mortification, mood or humour, quarrel, vapours, sombre thoughts. Bitterness, anger, spite.

Reversed: Surprise, enchantment, amazement or astonishment, confusion, embarrassment, distress or turmoil, unexpected event, unexpected action, fright, emotion, fear, terror or dread, frightening. Consternation, astonishment, domination, rapture or abduction, alarms. Wonder, phenomenon, miracle.

34
By Etteilla

Sadness

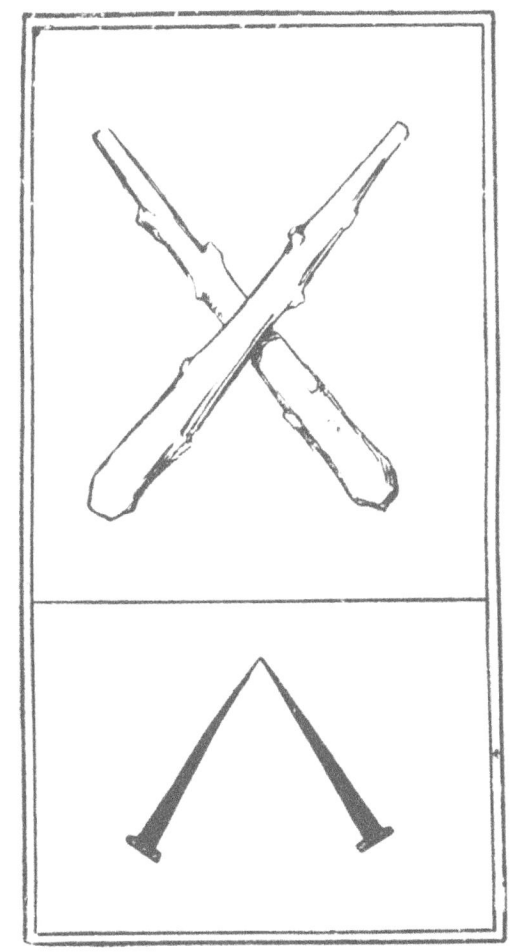

Sav-
iour's
help

March
10th to
20th

First
Quarter =
1st night

6.30 a.m.

Dark girl
child
from 2
to 4 years
old

BSNL

Surprise
TWO OF WANDS

Ace of Wands

Upright: From the point of view of spiritual healing, in its natural position, this card means: birth, beginning. Nativity, origin, creation. Source, principle or origin, primacy, primer. Extraction, race, family, condition, house, descendants, posterity, opportunity or occasion, cause, reason, first, premisses.

Reversed: Fall, cascade, decadence, decline, wasting away, pining, dwindling, withering or decay, diminishment, dissipation, insolvency, bankruptcy, ruin, destruction, demolition, damage, devastation or havoc. Fault, error, mistake or misunderstanding, exhaustion or despondency, dejection, discouragement. Perdition, abyss, chasm or depths, gulf, precipice. To perish, to fall, to demean (oneself), to wane, to fall from standing or to lose prestige, to derogate, detract or depreciate. Depth.

THE SEVENTY-EIGHT TAROT CARDS

35
By Etteilla

Birth

Towards initiation	1st to 10th March
Tarot Wheel	(month) First Quarter 1st day
The first principle	6 a.m. Dark infant 1 to 2 years old
	BNSL

Seeming victory
Be wary
Ace of Wands

King of Cups

Upright: From the point of view of spiritual healing, in its natural position, this card means: fair (haired) man, honest man, probity, equity or fairness, Art, Science.

Reversed: Man in a situation, distinguished man, honest man. Dishonest man. Exaction or extortion, embezzlement, injustice, brigand or bandit, thief, rogue or scamp. Vice, corruption, scandal.

36
By Etteilla

HE-YOD

THE MOTHER'S HUSBAND

KING OF CUPS

LAWYER

FAIR MAN

EFFEMINATE MAN

NB

KING OF CUPS

Queen of Cups

Upright: From the point of view of spiritual healing, in its natural position, this card means: fair (haired) woman. - Honest woman, virtue, wisdom, honesty.

Reversed: Woman of distinguished rank, honest woman. Vice, dishonesty, depravity, perversion or perverseness, disturbance, trouble or debauchery, corruption, scandal.

37
By Etteilla

HE-HE

HER OWN
MISTRESS

*Queen of
Cups*

Fair-haired
female
lawyer

Woman of
easy virtue

NN

QUEENS OF CUPS

Knight of Cups

Upright: From the point of view of spiritual healing, in its natural position, this card means: arrival, coming, approach, access, reception, admittance, rapprochement. Conformity Advent, approximation. Accession. Crowd. Comparison.

Reversed: Mischief, villainy, trickery, ruse, artifice. Finesse or refinement, adroitness, shrewdness or tact, versatility or pliability, cheating. Subtlety, irregularity. Wickedness or baseness.

38
By Etteilla

HE-VAU

CONQUEROR
OF
FORTUNE

KNIGHT OF
CUPS

AMOROUS
KNIGHT

ARRIVAL

NS

KNIGHT OF CUPS

Page of Cups

Upright: From the point of view of spiritual healing, in its natural position, this card means: fair-haired youth, studious. Study, application, work, reflection, observation, consideration, meditation, contemplation, occupation. Trade, profession, job.

Reversed: Penchant, fondness or weakness, tendency, propensity, inclination, attraction, taste, liking, passion, affection, attachment, friendship. Heart, urge, desire, attraction, commitment, seduction, invitation, charm or appeal. Flattery, cajolery, fawning or toadying, adulation, praise, credit. Inclined, threatening ruin, drawing to a close.

39
By Etteilla

HE-HE

SLAVE TO WOMANKIND

KING OF CUPS

FAIR YOUTH

MESSENGER OF LOVE

NL

PAGE OF CUPS

Ten of Cups

Upright: From the point of view of spiritual healing, in its natural position, this card means: town, city, homeland, country, market town, village, place, site, abode, house, residence. Citizen, townspeople, town dweller.

Reversed: Wrath, indignation, agitation, irritation, fit of anger, anger, violence.

40
By Etteilla

THE TOWN WHERE YOU ARE

31ST AUGUST TO 1ST SEPTEMBER

SECOND QUARTER = 7TH DAY

6 P.M.

BROTHER WITH WHOM TO BE UNITED
TEN OF CUPS

Nine of Cups

Upright: From the point of view of spiritual healing, in its natural position, this card means: victory, success, achievement, advantage, gain. Pomp, triumph, trophy, pre-eminence, superiority. Spectacle or show, trappings, equipment, paraphernalia or outfit.

Reversed: Sincerity, truth, reality, loyalty, good faith, frankness, ingenuousness, candour, open-heartedness, simplicity. Freedom, science, liberties, familiarity, boldness or audacity, ease, debauchery.

41
By Etteilla

Victory

Love
marriage

August 20ᵀᴴ to 30ᵀʜ

Full Moon = 6ᵀʜ day

5 p.m.

Sincerity
Nine of Cups

Eight of Cups

Upright: From the point of view of spiritual healing, in its natural position, this card means: fair-haired girl, practical girl, honour, propriety, modesty, reserve, timidity, fear, apprehension, gentleness or sweetness, charm or attractiveness.

Reversed: Satisfaction, well-being, contentment, gaiety, joy, happiness, rejoicing, fun, party. Excuse, reparation, exoneration. Public rejoicing, spectacle, equipment or paraphernalia, outfit, dressing, preparations, arrangement.

42
By Etteilla

Fair girl

Love of justice

August 10th to 20th

Full Moon = 5th day

4 p.m.

Full Moon

Celebration-gaiety
Eight of Cups

Seven of Cups

Upright: From the point of view of spiritual healing, in its natural position, this card means: thought, soul, mind, intelligence, idea, memory, imagination, understanding or comprehension, conception, meditation, contemplation, reflection, deliberation, view, opinion, feeling.

Reversed: Plan, design or outline, intention, desire, will, resolution, determination, premeditation.

43
BY ETTEILLA

THOUGHT

SCIENCE OF LOVE

AUGUST 1ST TO 10TH

FULL MOON = 4TH DAY

3 P.M.

PLANS
SEVEN OF CUPS

Six of Cups

Upright: From the point of view of spiritual healing, in its natural position, this card means: the past, the past tense, withered, faded. Formerly, earlier, previously, formerly, in the past, in the old days or once. Old age, decrepitude, antiquity.

Reversed: Future, prospective. After, next, later, further. Regeneration, resurrection. Reproduction, renewal or recurrence, reiteration.

44
By Etteilla

THE PAST

PATIENCE

JULY 20ᵀᴴ TO 30ᵀᴴ

FULL MOON = 3ᴿᴰ NIGHT

2.30 P.M.

THE FUTURE
SIX OF CUPS

Five of Cups

Upright: From the point of view of spiritual healing, in its natural position, this card means: inheritance, succession, legacy, gift, donation, dowry, heritage, handing down, will. Tradition, resolution. Kabbalah.

Reversed: Consanguinity, blood, family, forefathers, ancestors or forerunners, father, mother, brother, sister, uncle, aunt, male cousin, female cousin. Line of descent or affiliation, extraction, race, descendants or lineage, alliance. Affinity, contacts, relationship, liaisons.

45
By Etteilla

Heritage

July 10th to 20th

Full Moon = 3rd day

2 p.m.

Flawed plan
Five of Cups

Four of Cups

Upright: From the point of view of spiritual healing, in its natural position, this card means: boredom, displeasure, discontent, disgust, aversion, enmity, hatred, horror, worry, anxiety or concern, mental pain, slight sorrow, affliction, distressing, laborious or painful, unfortunate, tiresome, unpleasant. Distressing, lamentable or appalling.

Reversed: New teaching, new light. Sign, indication, conjecture. Omen, portent, premonitions, forecast or prognosis, prediction, novelty.

46
BY ETTEILLA

BOREDOM

Force for good

July 1ST to 10TH

Full Moon = 2ND night

1.30 P.M

NEW ACQUAINTANCE
FOUR OF CUPS

Three of Cups

Upright: From the point of view of spiritual healing, in its natural position, this card means: success, science, fortunate outcome, happy ending, victory. Recovery, cure, relief. Accomplishment. Perfection.

Reversed: Despatching or expedition, execution or performance, completion, end, conclusion, termination, accomplishment or fulfilment.

47
By Etteilla

Success

Good-
ness

June 20th
to 30th

Full
Moon =
2nd day

1 p.m.

Business trip
Three of Cups

Two of Cups

Upright: From the point of view of spiritual healing, in its natural position, this card means: love, passion, inclination, liking, appeal or fascination, propensity, friendship, benevolence, affection, attachment, taste, liaison, chivalry, attraction, affinity.

Reversed: Desire, wish, vow or pledge, will, urge, greed, lust or cupidity, concupiscence, jealousy or envy, passion, illusion, appetite.

48
BY ETTEILLA

LOVE

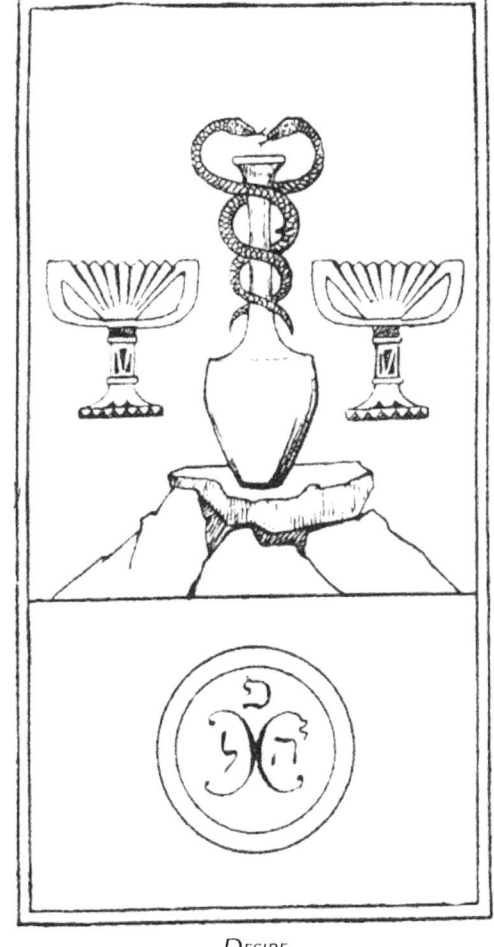

SALVA-
TION

JUNE 10ᵀᴴ
TO 20ᵀᴴ
JUNE

FULL
MOON =
1ˢᵗ NIGHT

12.30
P.M.

DESIRE
TWO OF CUPS

Ace of Cups

Upright: From the point of view of spiritual healing, in its natural position, this card means: table, meal, feast or banquet, gala, treat, nourishment, food, nutrition. Guests, services. Invitation, prayer or plea, petition, convocation or summons, notification, call-up. Host, hotel, hotel trade, inn. Abundance, fertility, production, solidity, stability, fixity, constancy, perseverance, continuation, duration, sequel, assiduity, persistence, steadfastness or firmness, courage. Picture, painting, image, hieroglyph, description. Tablets, note-case, wallet or portfolio, study, writing-desk. Nature's table, bronze table, marble table, law. Catalogue, table of contents. Sound-board, garden table, communion table.

Reversed: Transformation or mutation, permutation, transmutation, deterioration or adulteration, vicissitude, varieties, variation, inconstancy, frivolity, slightness, rashness, wantonness, irresponsibility, casualness or thoughtlessness, exchange, barter, purchase, sale, market, deal or transaction, treaty, convention. Metamorphosis, diversity, versatility, reversal, disruption, upheaval or upset, revolution, reversion. Version, translation, interpretation.

49
By Etteilla

TABLE

LOVE

JUNE 1ST TO 10TH

FULL MOON = 1ST DAY

MIDDAY

CHANGE
ACE OF CUPS

King of Swords

Upright: From the point of view of spiritual healing, in its natural position, this card means: man of the cloth, gownsman, judge, councillor, assessor, senator, businessman, practitioner, lawyer, solicitor, doctor, physician. Jurist, jurisprudence. Litigant, jurisconsult.

Reversed: Ill-intentioned, malice, spite or nastiness, perversity, treachery, crime, cruelty, atrocity, inhumanity.

50
By Etteilla

VAU-IOD

THE
PRINCE
OF LOVE

KING OF
SWORDS

WARRIOR,
MAN OF
ACTION

MAN OF
JUSTICE

DARK OR
RED-HAIRED
MAN

SB

KING OF SWORDS

Queen of Swords

Upright: From the point of view of spiritual healing, in its natural position, this card means: widowhood or widowerhood, viduity, deprivation, absence, shortage or lack, sterility, indigence or destitution, poverty. Empty, vacant, unoccupied, idle, unproductive, free.

Reversed: Bad woman. Cruelty or spite, malice, treachery, deceit, cheating, swindle or double-dealing, finesse, subtlety, keenness, sharpness, refinement or delicacy, artifice, mischievousness or prank, bigotry, prudery, hypocrisy.

51
By Etteilla

VAU-HE

PRINCESS
OF LOVE

QUEEN OF
SWORDS

WOMAN
OF ACTION

WIDOW
OR WOMAN
ACTING ON
HER OWN
BEHALF

SN

QUEENS OF SWORDS

Knight of Swords

Upright: From the point of view of spiritual healing, in its natural position, this card means: soldier, swordsman, man of arms, master of fencing, hired assassin, hired ruffian or bully. Soldier from any corps and skilled in the use of any weapon, combatant, enemy. Dispute, war, combat, battle, duel. Attack, defence, opposition, resistance, destruction, ruin, reversal, overthrow or change of direction. Enmity, hatred, anger, resentment. Courage, valour, bravery or gallantry. Henchman or satellite.

Reversed: Incompetence, ineptitude, stupidity or foolishness, idiocy, folly or foolish trifle, imprudence, impertinence, extravagance, unreasonableness or eccentricity, ridiculousness, inanity or nonsense. Swindle, fraud, roguishness or mischievousness, industry.

52
By Etteilla

VAU-VAU

Con-
queror
in love

Knight of
Swords

Soldier

SS

KNIGHT OF SWORDS

Page of Swords

Upright: From the point of view of spiritual healing, in its natural position, this card means: spy, inquisitive person or onlooker, observer, scrutineer, dedicated person, amateur, or enthusiast, overseer, administrator, steward or bailiff. Examination, note, remark or comment, observation, annotation, speculation, account or bill, calculation, estimation or computation. – Scholar, artist.

Reversed: Unexpected, sudden, suddenly, like a bolt out of the blue. Astonishing, surprising, unexpectedly. To improvise, to act or to speak without preparation, to compose and recite on the spot.

53
By Etteilla

YOD-HE

Slave of Love

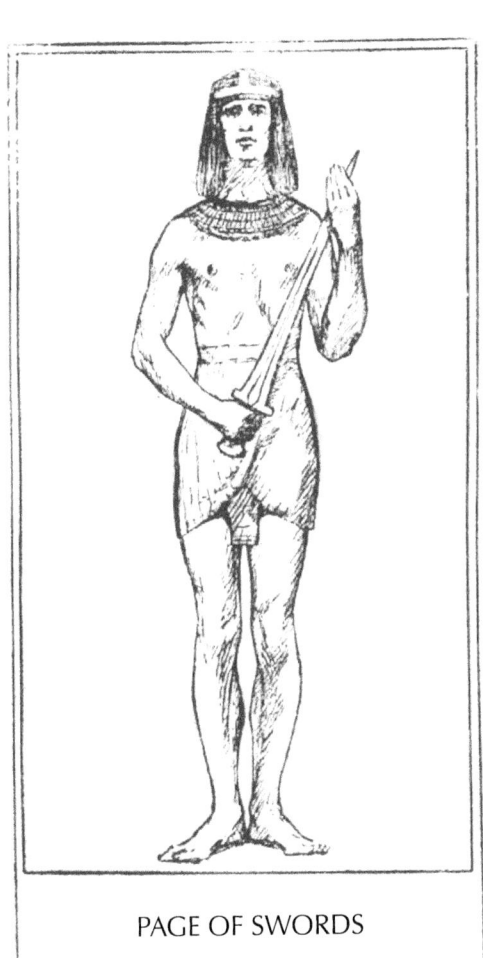

Page of Swords

Enemy envoy

SL

PAGE OF SWORDS

Ten of Swords

Upright: From the point of view of spiritual healing, in its natural position, this card means: weeping, tears, sobs, moans or groans, sighs, complaints, lamentations, grievances, diseases or disorders, sorrows, sadness, pain, wailing, lay, desolation.

Reversed: Advantage, gain, profit, success. Grace, favour, benefit. Ascendant, power, empire, authority, force, usurpation.

54
BY ETTEILLA
FLOWERS

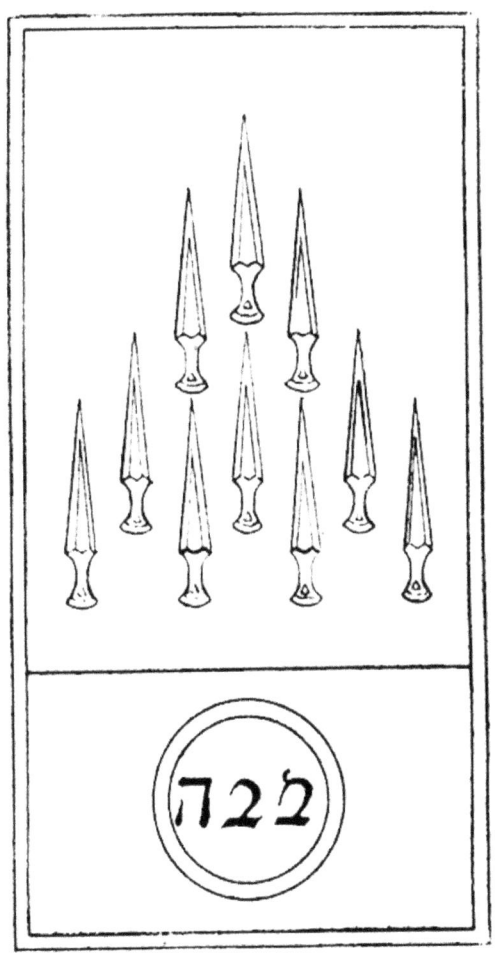

DECEMBER 1ST

SECOND QUARTER = 7TH DAY

MIDNIGHT

UNFORTUNATE EVENT THAT TURNS TO ADVANTAGE
TEN OF SWORDS

Nine of Swords

Upright: From the point of view of spiritual healing, in its natural position, this card means: celibate, celibacy, virginity, abbot, priest, monk or other male religious devotee, hermit, nun. Temple, church, monastery, convent, hermitage, sanctuary. Cult, religion, piety, devotion, rite, ceremony, ritual. Male recluse, female recluse, anchorite, vestal.

Reversed: Justified mistrust, well-founded suspicion, legitimate fear, distrust, doubt, conjecture. Scruple, god-fearing conscience, pure, timidity, propriety. Disgrace, shame.

55
By Etteilla

Man of the cloth

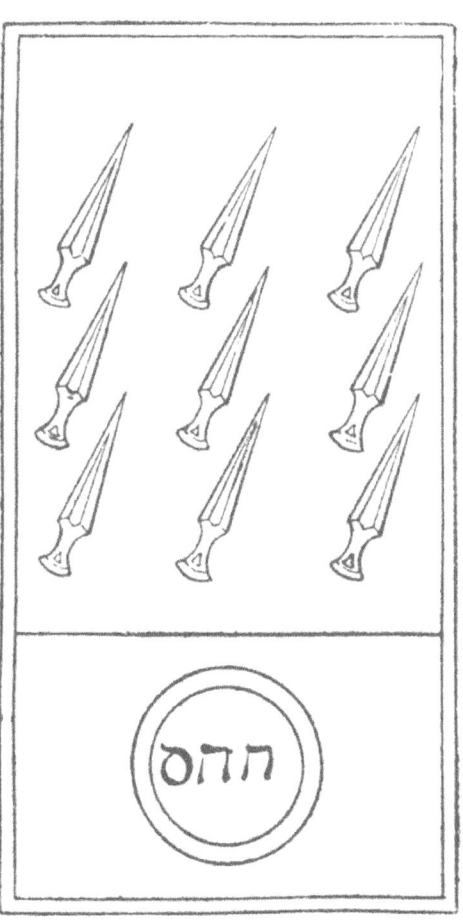

Triumph of strength

November 20th to 30th

Second Quarter = 6th day

11 p.m.

Be wary or justifiable wariness
Nine of Swords

Eight of Swords

Upright: From the point of view of spiritual healing, in its natural position, this card means: criticism, unfortunate position, critical moment, critical time, decisive moment, bad situation, delicate circumstances, crisis. Examination, discussion, search, pursuit, quest or research, blame, censure, gossip, conclusion, dénouement or epilogue, control, disapproval, condemnation, annulment or reduction to the ranks, judgement, contempt.

Reversed: Incident, difficulty, particular circumstance, conjunction, event, incidental, thoughtless, obstacle, delay, delayed action. Abjectness. Contestation, contradiction, opposition, resistance, chicanery, quibbling or squabbling. Unexpected, unforeseen, fortuitous event, adventure, occurrence, destiny, fatality, accidents, misfortunes, mishaps or hardships, disfavour, fall from grace or disgrace, misfortune, symptom or sign.

56
By Etteilla

Damage

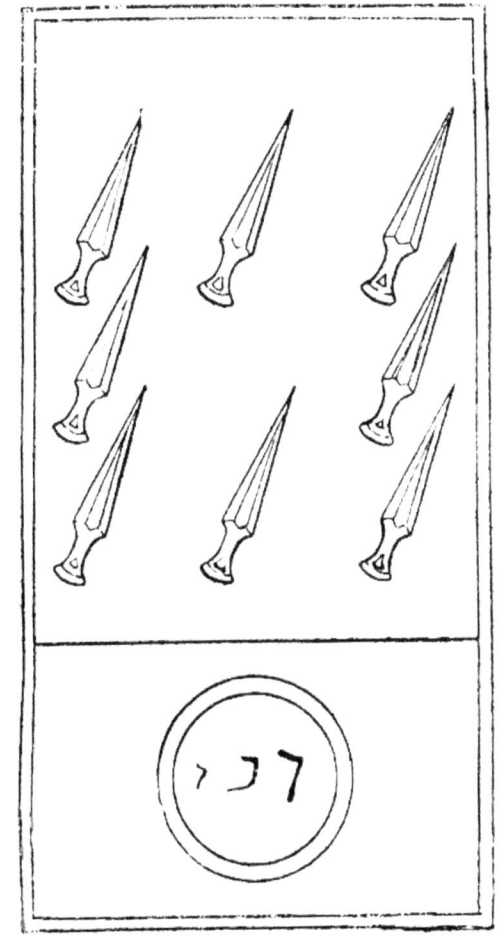

Balance of material force

November 10th to 20th

Second Quarter = 5th day

10 p.m.

Past betrayal
Eight of Swords

Seven of Swords

Upright: From the point of view of spiritual healing, in its natural position, this card means: hope, expectation, confidence, to claim or to intend, to have grounds or a basis for, to overestimate oneself, core, nub or foundation, intention, goal or purpose, will, to want, wish, vow, desire, taste, fantasy or imagination.

Reversed: Wise opinion, good advice, salutary warnings, instruction, lesson. Observation, reflection, remark or comment, notification, thought. Reprimand, reproach. News, announcement, notice or poster. Consultation, admonishment.

57
BY ETTEILLA

HOPE

VICTORY

NOVEMBER
1ST TO 10TH

SECOND
QUARTER =
4TH DAY

9 P.M.
(21)

WISE ADVICE
SEVEN OF SWORDS

Six of Swords

Upright: Route, alley, lane, footpath or avenue, way, course, passage, path, road. March or walk, traffic, gait, attentiveness, kindness or consideration, driving or steering, means, manner, fashion, expedient, race, career, walk, example, track, trail or trace, remnants, envoy, agent.

Reversed: Declaration, incorporation, development, explanation, interpretation. Charter, constitution, diploma, law, order or decree. Publication or promulgation, proclamation, openness or ostensibility, public notice or poster, publicity, authenticity, notoriety. Denunciation or accusation, counting or count. Enumeration. Acquaintance, discovery, unveiling or disclosure, vision, revelation, appearance or arrival, look, air or appearance, recognition or admission, confession, protestation, approval, authorisation.

58
By Etteilla

Envoy, Messenger

Harmony

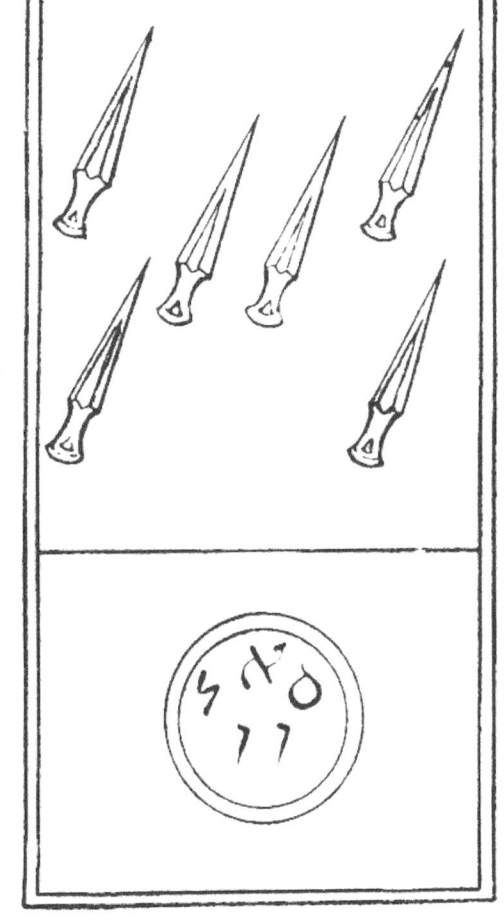

October 20th to 30th

Second Quarter = 3rd night

8.30 p.m

Declaration of love
Six of Swords

Five of Swords

Upright: In its natural position, this card means: loss, adulteration, falsification, distortion or alteration, waste matter or scraps, degradation, wastage or loss, fading away, wasting away or decline, destruction, deterioration, detriment, diminution or alleviation, harm, injuries or damages, failure or checkmate, prejudice, defect or loss of value, wrong, avarice, decline in business, damage, disadvantage, devastation, dilapidation, dissipation, misfortune, mishap or unhappiness, reversal, setback, ruin.Defeat, retreat. Debauchery, shame, defamation, dishonour, infamy, ignominy, affront, ugliness, deformity, humiliation. Theft or robbery, petty larceny, abduction, plagiarism, removal, hideous, horrible. Opprobrium, corruption, disturbance or upset, seduction, libertinage.

Reversed: Mourning, despondency, disorder or disease, sorrow, pain, suffering, funeral parlour, funeral procession, state funeral, funeral, burial, burial place, tomb or entombment.

59
By Etteilla

Loss

The New Jerusalem

October 10th to 20th

Second Quarter = 3rd day

8 p.m.

Mourning
Five of Swords

Four of Swords

Upright: From the point of view of spiritual healing, in its natural position, this card means: solitude, desert, retreat, hermitage. Exile, banishment, proscription. Uninhabited, isolated, abandoned, forsaken or neglected. Tomb or grave, sepulchre, coffin.

Reversed: Economy, good conduct, wise administration. Foresight or providence, management, household or housekeeping, savings, avarice. Order, arrangement, relationship, suitability, entente, agreement, similarity, harmony, music, disposition or layout. Testament. Reservation, restriction, exception. Circumspection, restraint or self-control, wisdom, friendship, fellow feeling or sympathy, thoughtfulness, precaution.

60
By Etteilla

Solitude

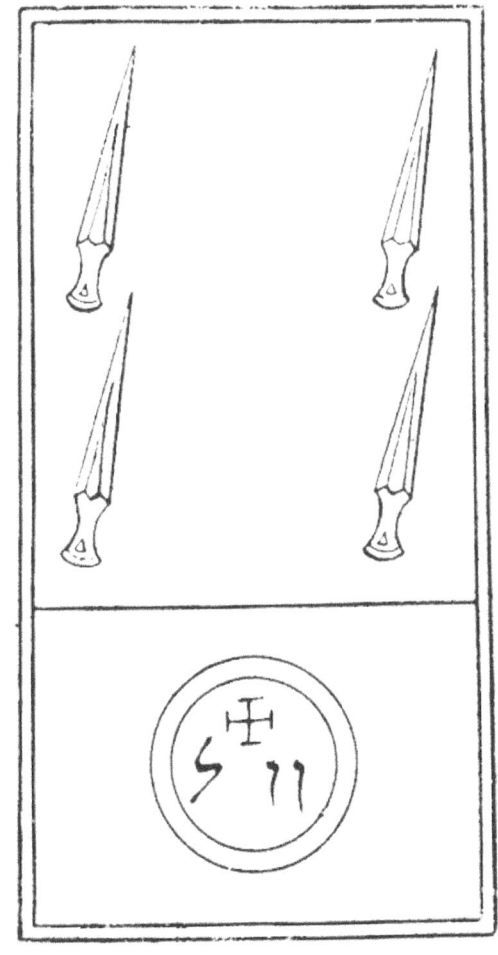

Clear light of glass

October 1ST to 10TH

Second Quarter = 2ND night

7.30 P.M

Economy
Four of Swords

Three of Swords

Upright: From the point of view of spiritual healing, in its natural position, this card means: distance, departure, absence, difference or deviation, dispersion, distant, faraway or remote, delay. –Disdain, repugnance, aversion, hatred, disgust, horror. Incompatibility, vexation or clash, opposition, unsociability, misanthropy, discourteousness. – Separation, division, rupture, antipathy, section, cut or cutting.

Reversed: Distraction, insanity or dementia, rambling, mental illness, absent-mindedness, wild or crazy behaviour. – Error, disappointment or disillusionment, loss, curve or detour, difference or discrepancy, dispersion, dispersal or scattering.

61
BY ETTEILLA

Nun

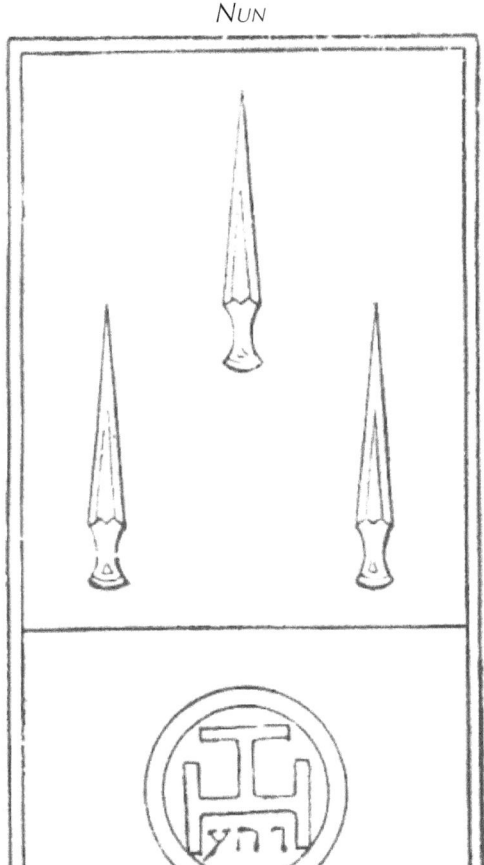

September 20TH to 30TH

Second Quarter = 2ND day

7.30 P.M.

Wild effet
THREE OF SWORDS

Two of Swords

Upright: From the point of view of spiritual healing, in its natural position, this card means: friendship, attachment, affection, tenderness, benevolence, rapport, relationship, identity, intimacy, suitability, correspondence, interest, conformity, friendship, fellow feeling or sympathy, affinity, attraction.

Reversed: False, falseness, lie, fraud, duplicity, bad faith, deception, trick or hoax, dissimulation, treachery, deception, superficial, area, surface.

62
By Etteilla

Friendship

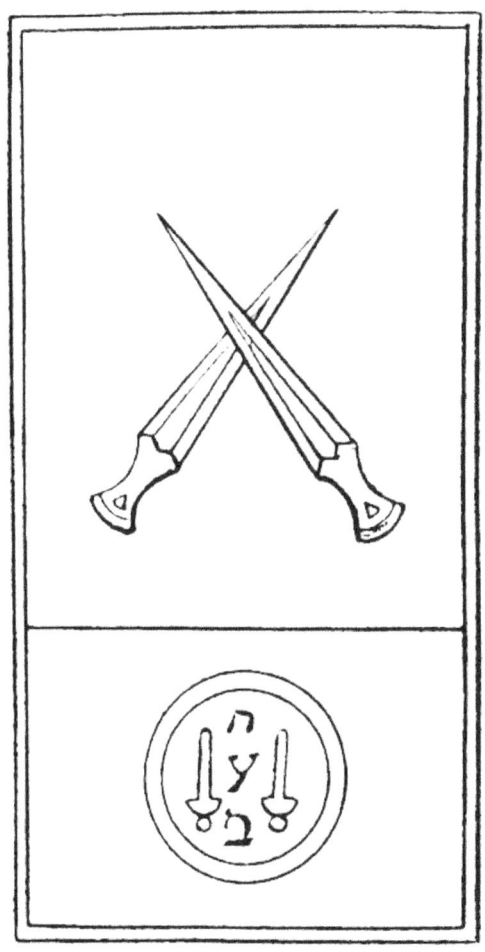

Political equilibrium

September 10th to 20th

Second Quarter = 1st night

6.30 p.m.

False friends or friends who are little help Relatives of little help
Two of Swords

Ace of Swords

Upright: From the point of view of spiritual healing, in its natural position, this card means: extreme, large, excessive. Exaggerated, furious or overwhelming, quick-tempered. Extremely, passionately, excessively. Vehemence, animosity, transport or outburst, fit of anger, anger, violent passion, rage or mania. Extremity, borders, confines, tip, limits. Last breath, farthest extremity. Misunderstanding or disagreement.

Reversed: Pregnancy, germ, seed or semen, sperm, matter, making pregnant, generating or breeding, conception, fructification, labour or delivery, childbirth. Fertilisation, production, composition. Enlargement, increase, multiplicity.

63
By Etteilla

Mad passionate love

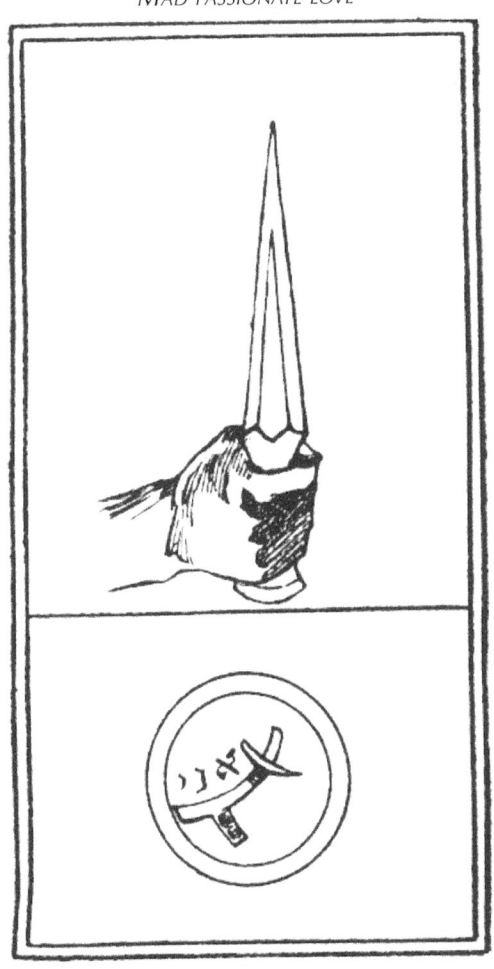

September
1ST TO 10TH

Second
Quarter
=1ST DAY

6 P.M.

Pregnancy
Ace of Swords

King of Coins

Upright: From the point of view of spiritual healing, in its natural position, this card means: dark man, merchant, trader or wholesaler, banker, stockbroker, shrewd operator, speculator. Physics, geometry, mathematics, science. Master, professor or teacher.

Reversed: Vice, fault, weakness, defectiveness, defective structure, amorphousness Disturbance or upset, ugliness, deformity. Corruption. Stench.

64
By Etteilla

The father creator

King of Coins

Man of the interior

Man with light brown hair

Trader

LB

KING OF COINS

Queen of Coins

Upright: From the point of view of spiritual healing, in its natural position, this card means: dark woman, opulence, wealth, splendour, luxury, sumptuousness. Assurance, reliability, confidence, certainty, affirmation. Safety or security, boldness, freedom, frankness.

Reversed: Unsure, doubting, uncertain, doubt, indecision, uncertainty. Fear, alarm, fright, timidity, apprehension, vacillation, hesitation. Indeterminate, irresolute, perplexed or puzzled, in suspense.

65
By Etteilla

Teacher of children

Queen of Coins

Woman of the interior

Trader

Rich woman

LN

QUEES OF COINS

Knight of Coins

Upright: From the point of view of spiritual healing, in its natural position, this card means: Useful, advantage, gain, profit, interest. Profitable, interesting, advantageous, important, necessary, obliging, unofficial or informal.

Reversed: Peace, tranquillity, rest, sleep, apathy, inertia, stagnation, inactivity, idleness. Leisure, pastime. Recreation, carefreeness, nonchalance, indolence, sloth, laziness, numbness, sluggishness or torpor, discouragement, annihilation or destruction.

66
By Etteilla

Con-
queror
of works

Knight of
Coins

Traveller

Helpful
man

LS

KNIGHT OF COINS

Page of Coins

Upright: From the point of view of spiritual healing, in its natural position, this card means: dark-haired boy, study, education, training or instruction, application, meditation, reflection. Work, employment, apprenticeship. schoolboy, follower, disciple, pupil, apprentice, enthusiast or amateur, student, speculator, trader.

Reversed: Profession, superfluity, largesse or bounty, luxury, sumptuousness, magnificence, abundance, multiplicity. Liberality, benefit, generosity, charity or beneficence. Crowd, multitude. Degradation, dilapidation, pillage, dissipation.

67
By Etteilla

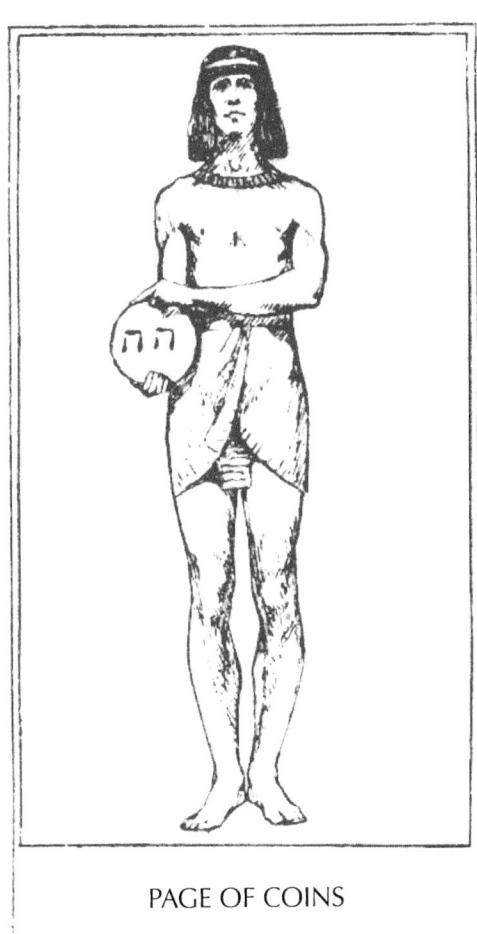

Slave of works

Servant of children or groups

Page of Coins

Envoy of friends

Money courier

LL

PAGE OF COINS

Ten of Coins

Upright: From the point of view of spiritual healing, in its natural position, this card means: house, household, economy, savings. Dwelling or abode, domicile, habitation, manor, lodgings, regiment, building, ship, vase, vessel or receptacle. Archive, château or castle, thatched cottage. Family, extraction, race, posterity. Cave or lair, cavern, den or haunt.

Reversed: Prize, fortune, game, accident or act of God, chance, ignorance, lot, fate, destiny, mischance or fatality. Happy or unhappy occasion.

68
By Etteilla

The House

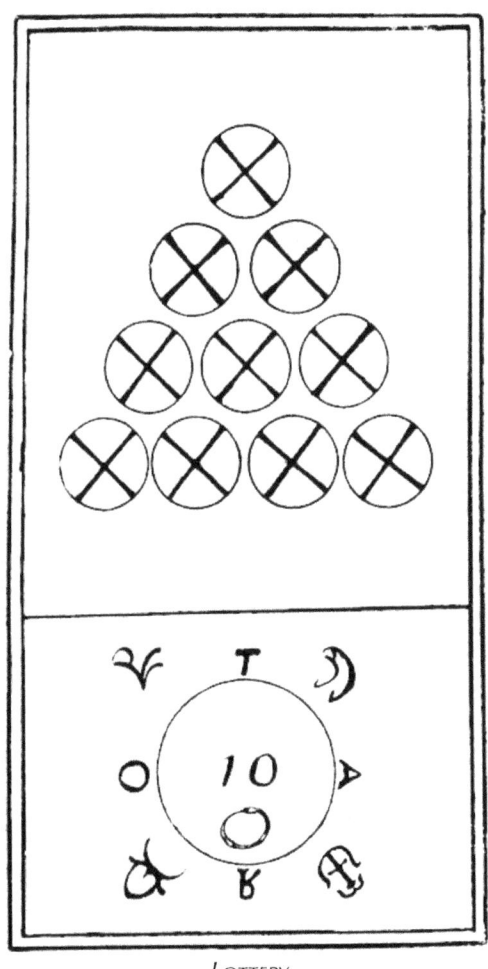

29ᵀᴴ FEBRUARY
1ˢᵀ MARCH
(LEAP YEAR)

NEW
MOON =
7ᵀᴴ DAY

FIRST
QUARTER =
6 A.M.

Lottery
TEN OF COINS

Nine of Coins

Upright: From the point of view of spiritual healing, in its natural position, this card means: effect, realisation, positive, accomplishment, success.

Reversed: Dupery, swindle or fraud, deception, promises, to no effect, vain hopes, aborted plans.

69
By Etteilla

Effect

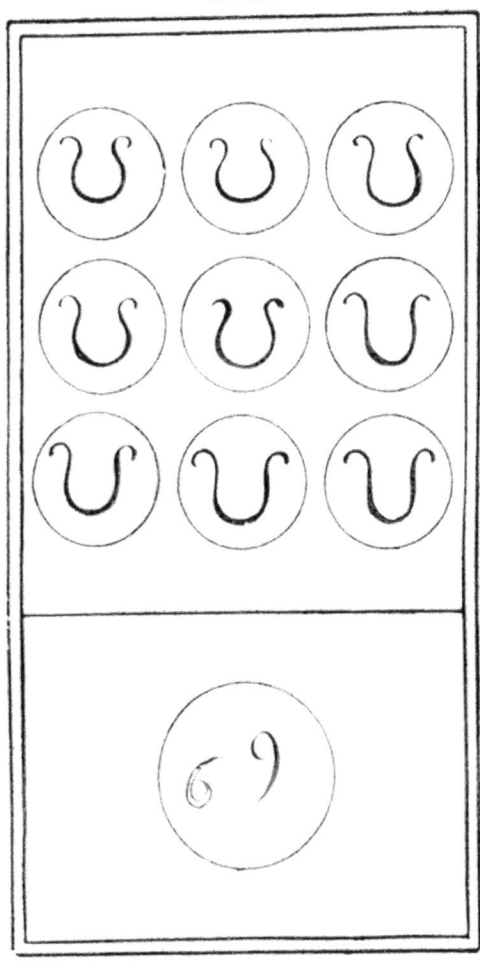

Sublimation of Compounds

February 20ᵀᴴ to 28ᵀᴴ

New Moon = 6ᵀᴴ day

5 a.m

Deception
Nine of Coins

Eight of Coins

Upright: From the point of view of spiritual healing, in its natural position, this card means: dark-haired girl, passive, depths of night.

Reversed: Yearning for the void, avarice, usury.

70
By Etteilla

Dark girl

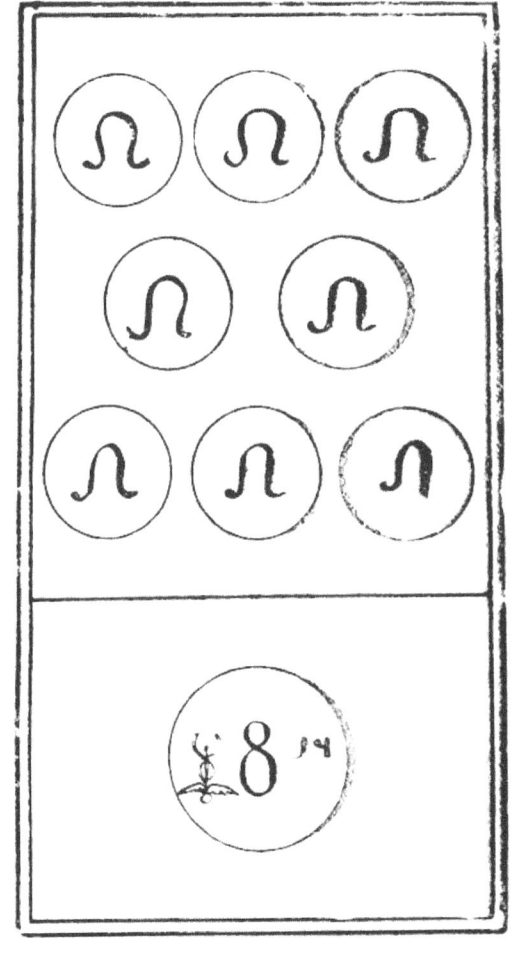

Justice incarnate

February 10th to 20th

New Moon = 5th day

4 a.m.

Money lending
Eight of Coins

Seven of Coins

Upright: From the point of view of spiritual healing, in its natural position, this card means: money, wealth, sum, coin. Silverware. Whiteness, parity, candour, innocence, ingenuousness, moon. Purging, purification.

Reversed: Worry, agony of mind, impatience, affliction, sadness, concern, solicitude, care, attention, diligence, application. Apprehension, fear, mistrust, wariness, suspicion.

71
By Etteilla

Money

MATERIAL VICTORY

FEBRUARY
1ST TO 10TH

NEW MOON = 4TH DAY

3 A.M.

Worries
SEVEN OF COINS

Six of Coins

Upright: From the point of view of spiritual healing, in its natural position, this card means: currently, presently, now, incontinent, suddenly, instantly, right now, today, assistant, witness, contemporary. Attentive, careful, vigilant.

Reversed: Desire, wish, ardour, eagerness, passion, quest, cupidity or greed, desire, jealousy, illusion.

72
By Etteilla

The present

Balance of compounds

January 20ᵀᴴ to 30ᵀᴴ

New Moon = 3ᴿᴰ night

2.30 a.m.

Ambition
Six of Coins

Five of Coins

Upright: From the point of view of spiritual healing, in its natural position, this card means: lover, mistress, sweetheart, ladies' man, woman of easy virtue, husband, wife, newly-wed man, newly-wed woman, male friend, female friend. Enthusiast. To love, to cherish, to adore. Matching, agreement, suitability or affinity, eligibility, decorum or propriety.

Reversed: Disorderly, countermand. Misconduct, trouble, confusion, chaos. Damage, devastation, ruin. Dissipation, consumption. Disturbance or upset, libertinage. dissension, disharmony, discord.

73
By Etteilla

Lover or Master

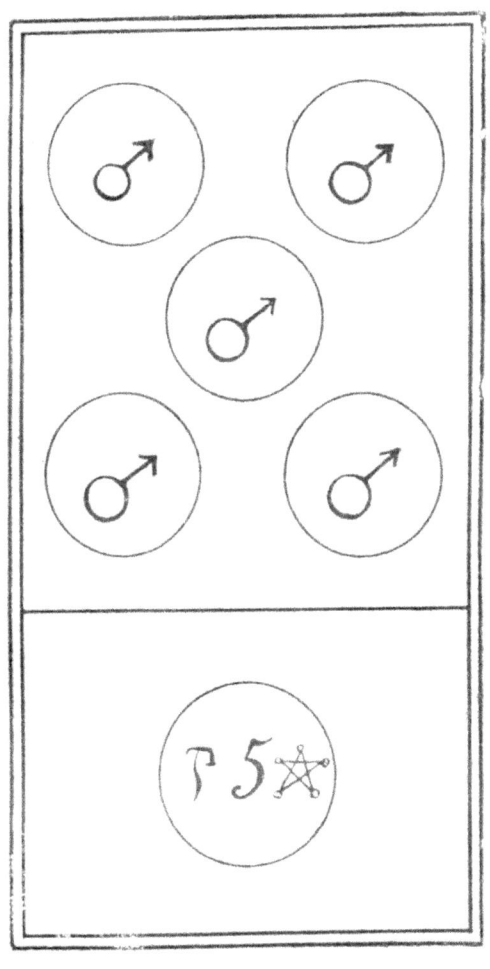

Blending of compounds

January 10ᵀᴴ to 20ᵀᴴ

New Moon = 3ᴿᴰ day

2 a.m.

Lack of Order
Five of Coins

Four of Coins

Upright: From the point of view of spiritual healing, in its natural position, this card means: present, gift, generosity, benefit, liberality, Christmas box or Christmas bonus, favour, offering, donation, tip or bonus, service. The colour white, lunar medicine, White Stone.

Reversed: Enclosure, circuit, circumvolution, circumscription or district, circumference, circle, circulation or traffic. To intercept, obstruction, saturation, hoarding or monopolising, cloister, monastery, convent. Halted, stopped or discontinued, fixed or set, determined, final, definitive or conclusive, extremity, bounds, limits, terms, end, barrier, partition, wall, hedge, partition wall or inner face. – Obstacles, bars, prevention, suspension, delay, opposition.

74
By Etteilla

IT'S A GIFT

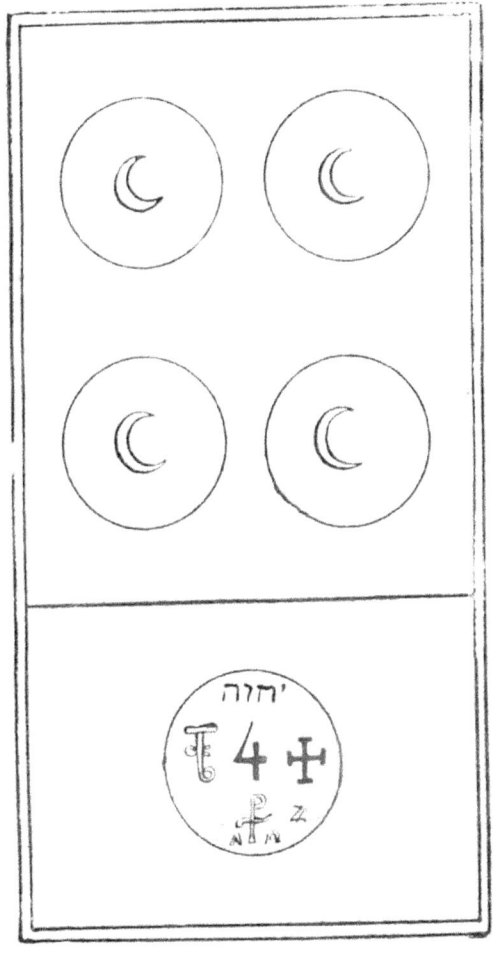

MATER-
ALISATION
OF FLUIDS

JANUARY
1ST TO 10TH

NEW
MOON =
2ND NIGHT

1.30 A.M.

CLOSURE
FOUR OF COINS

Three of Coins

Upright: From the point of view of spiritual healing, in its natural position, this card means: noble, important, famous, great, major, reach or expanse, vast, sublime, renowned, famous, powerful, elevated, illustrious. Illustration, consideration, greatness of soul, nobleness of deeds, generous actions, magnificently, splendidly.

Reversed: Puerility, childhood, childishness, frivolity. Weakening, abasement or lowering, politeness, lowness or smallness, mediocrity, meticulousness or intricacy, trinket, trifle or bagatelle, frivolity, baseness, cowardice, faint-heartedness, offspring or offshoot, little one, puerile, sickly, low, creeping or crawling, vile, abject, humble. Abjection, humility, humiliation.

75
By Etteilla

Nobility

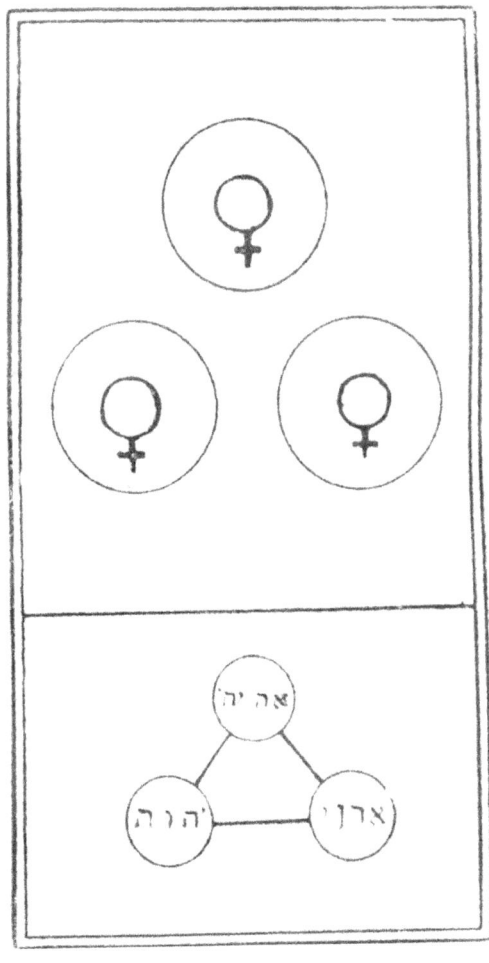

Hermetic balance

December 20th to 30th

New Moon = 2nd day

1 a.m.

Child
Three of Coins

Two of Coins

Upright: From the point of view of spiritual healing, in its natural position, this card means: difficulty, obstacle, clash, obstruction, hitch, snag. Trouble, worry, shock or fright, sowing discord, confusion, difficulty, prevention, twisting or entangling, obscurity. Agitation, anxiety, perplexity, solicitude.

Reversed: Note, document, writing, text, literature, doctrine, erudition, work, book, production, composition. News, epistle, missive. Letter of the alphabet or character. Literal meaning. Alphabet, elements, principles, bill of exchange.

76
BY ETTEILLA

EMBARRASSMENT/ AWKWARD POSITION/ CONFUSION

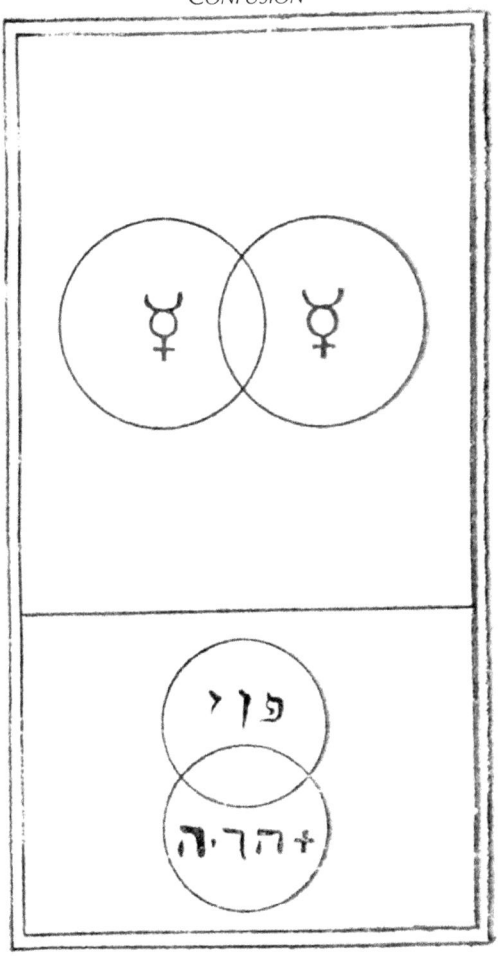

MATERAIAL OPPOSITION

DECEMBER 10TH TO 20TH

NEW MOON = 1ST NIGHT

HALF PAST MIDNIGHT

LETTER
TWO OF COINS

Ace of Coins

Upright: From the point of view of spiritual healing, in its natural position, this card means: perfect contentment, happiness, well-being, rapture, enchantment, ecstasy, wonder, complete satisfaction, total joy, inexpressible pleasure, the colour red, perfect medicine, solar medicine, pure, accomplished.

Reversed: Sum, capital, principle. Treasure, wealth, opulence. Rare, dear, precious, inestimable.

77
By Etteilla

PERFECT CONTENTMENT

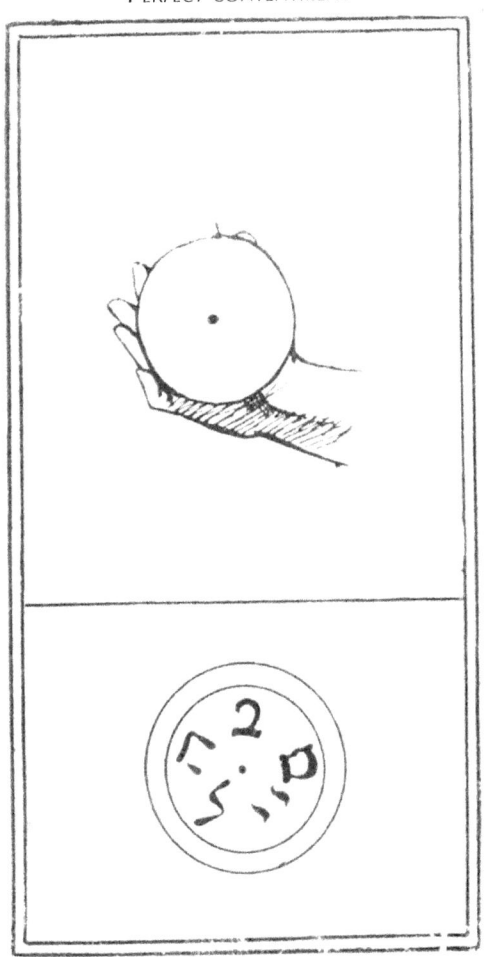

UNI-
VERSAL
MATTER

DECEMBER
1ST TO 10TH

NEW
MOON =
1ST DAY

MIDNIGHT

PURSE OF MONEY
ACE OF COINS

CHAPTER THREE

Drawing and reading tarot cards

THE MAJOR ARCANA—DIVINATORY MEANINGS

The major arcana consist of 22 symbolic cards. We have yet to study them from the point of view of divination.

The meanings of the cards are quite easy to remember if you take the trouble to look at the descriptions carefully one by one. In addition, here is a general rule which will act as a further memory aid. The first seven cards are mainly about man's intellectual side, the seven after that are about his moral side and the last seven are about the various events that occur in his life. Having said this, let us set out the meanings of the 22 major cards in the Tarot deck:

1. The Mountebank means: the male querent
2. The High Priestess: the female querent
3. The Empress: Action. Initiative.
4. The Emperor: Will.
5. The High Priest: Inspiration.
6. The Lover: Love.
7. The Chariot: Triumph. Protection through divine providence.
8. Justice: Justice.
9. The Hermit: Prudence.
10. The Wheel of Fortune: Fortune. Destiny.
11. Strength: Strength.
12. The Hanged Man: Ordeal. Sacrifice.
13. Death: Death.
14. Temperance: Temperance. Economy.
15. The Devil: Force majeure. Illness.
16. The House of God: Ruin. Deception.
17. The Star: Hope.
18. The Moon: Concealed enemies. Danger.
19. The Sun: Material good fortune. Fertile marriage.
20. Judgement: Change of position
21. The Fool: Impulse. Folly.
22. The World: Guaranteed success.

The Basis for Applying the Above Information

You are now in a position to be able to use the Tarot for divination. But before embarking on this subject, it is essential to establish the system to be followed when laying out the cards. For knowing the meanings of the cards is only the first part of the art of cartomancy. It is even more important to know how to position them. As I have already pointed out, Tarot is not supposed to be used for any other purpose than astronomical information and representation of the movements of the stars as the source of future events. However, such things belong to the sphere of astrology, and the idea here is to confine ourselves to drawing Tarot spreads governed by chance.

Nevertheless, I shall be setting out as many practical elements as possible in this study. For example, if you refer back to the beginning of this third part—Key to the Applications of Tarot—it is clear to see that human life goes through four major phases of development known as:

Childhood
Youth
Maturity
Old age

If you are not concerned with a human life but simply wish to look at the development of an event, the latter will also pass through four major stages, namely:

Beginning
Zenith
Decline
Nadir

So, first, we must first determine four opposite points in the space to be occupied by the cards, and these are the positions where we will place the cards that are going to reveal the future. The first stage of the process is now firmly established, namely, determining the four positions where the cards are to be laid.

4
Zenith
Youth

1 Beginning Childhood		3 Decline Ripening years

2
Fall
Old age

Note that the arrangement of the points goes from left to right as per the order of the numbers, whereas the symbols are read from right to left.

Human life and events pass through three clearly distinguishable periods:

> Past
> Present
> Future

and this gives us the following new configuration:

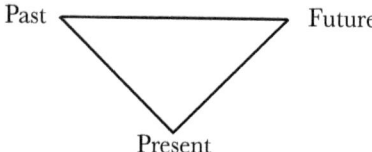

The card representing the querent is placed at the centre of this configuration. The arrangement of the triangle follows the order of the numbers, not that of the symbols.

However, since four points are not enough to provide an exact reproduction of the course of the Sun across the sky, for large Tarot spreads we shall use twelve points corresponding to the twelve months of the year. The resulting configuration—set out as follows—is for use when drawing cards about the major events in life. But it can also be used to consult the Tarot about minor events.

It is extremely important to make a thorough study of this figure, which is composed of three circles:

1. The outer circle consisting of twelve spaces to be filled by minor arcana, and arranged according to the numbering as shown from left to right;
2. The middle circle consisting of four spaces arranged from right to left;
3. The inner circle marked by the triangle, and containing one space at each point of the triangle, which amounts to a total of three spaces.

DRAWING AND READING TAROT CARDS

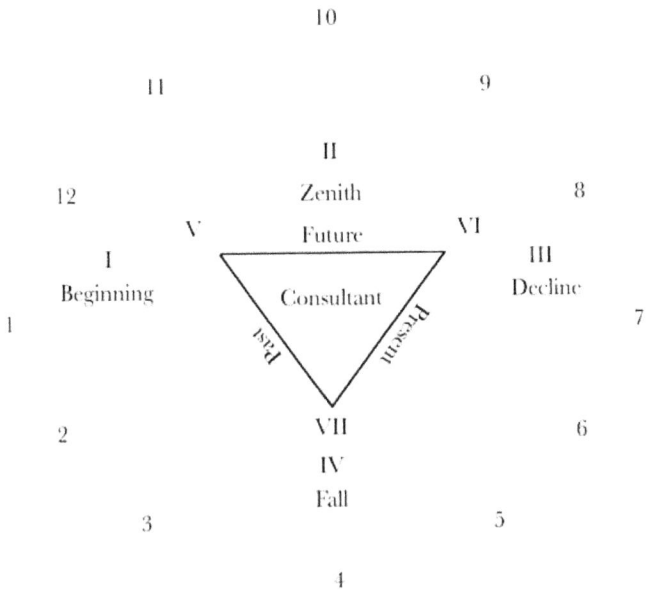

The inner and middle circles are to be filled with major arcana.

At the very centre of the configuration will be the male or female querent, depending on the case in question.

Drawing Tarot Cards

I—Quick method:

Suppose you need to draw a horoscope for any given matter. How do you go about it?

1. Take the minor arcana and separate out the whole of the suit relating to the type of question asked.
   If it is a business matter the querent is about to embark upon, take the Wands.
   If it is an affair of the heart, take the Cups.

174   THE DIVINATORY TAROT

If it is a legal matter or any kind of conflict, take the Swords.
If it is a money matter, take the Coins.

2. Shuffle the chosen stack of cards, then ask the querent to cut them.
3. Take the top four cards from the stack. Then without looking at them, arrange them from left to right in the shape of a cross according to the numbered positions shown below.

```
                    4

       3                           1

                    2
```

4. Take the major arcana (which must be kept separate from the minor arcana throughout), shuffle them and ask the querent to cut them.
5. Get the querent to choose seven cards from among the major arcana at random, and hand them to you without looking at them.
6. Shuffle these seven cards and ask the querent to cut them, then take the top three cards from the stack. Without looking at them, arrange them in a triangle in the following order:

```
       I                           II

                   III
```

This will give you the following configuration:

```
                    4 (Minor Arcana)

         I (Major Arcana)      (Major Arcana) II

1 (Minor Arcana)                           3 (Minor Arcana)

                    III (Major Arcana)

                    2 (Minor Arcana)
```

8. Turn the cards over so that you can see them, then read the meanings of the oracles, bearing in mind that the card in position 1 marks the beginning.
   The card in position 2 indicates the zenith, the one in position 3 indicates the obstacles and the one in position 4 indicates the fall.
   The major arcanum in position I indicates past influences on the matter in hand.
   The major arcanum in position II indicates factors influencing the situation at present.
   Lastly, the major arcanum in position III shows those factors which will influence and determine the future.

These processes take no time at all once you are used to them. It is important to note that, when the cards are drawn according to this quick procedure, the figures no longer represent people with a particular hair colour. Instead, the King represents a man with no other distinguishing features, the Queen a woman, the Knight a young man and the Page a child.

II—FULL PROCEDURE

1. Shuffle the minor arcana and ask the querent to cut them.
2. Take the top twelve cards from the stack and place them in a circle as follows:

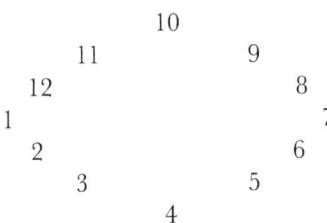

3. Shuffle the major arcana and ask the querent to cut them. Ask the querent to choose seven cards.
4. Take the top four cards from this stack and arrange them as follows, inside the cards in positions 1, 10, 7 and 4:

176 THE DIVINATORY TAROT

```
              II

      I              III

             IV
```

5. And, finally, place the last three cards in a triangle at the centre of the figure in the following positions:

```
      V              VI

             VII
```

You now have the following general configuration as shown earlier in the chapter:

Place the querent card at the centre of the figure if this has not already appeared from among the cards drawn. If the querent card – male or female – has been drawn, place it in the middle and replace it with a fresh card drawn by the querent from the major arcana.

The 12 minor arcana indicate the different phases through which

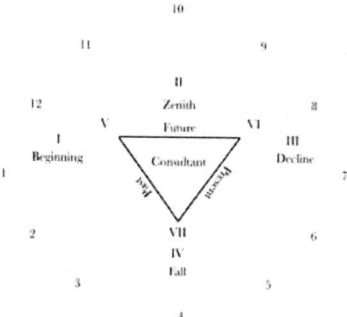

the life of the individual passes, or the development of the event during the four main phases.

Major arcanum I indicates the beginning and the nature of the beginning, arcanum II shows the zenith, arcana III the decline or the presence of obstacles and arcanum IV the fall.

Lastly, the three major arcana in the centre indicate special features of the horoscope in the Past (V), the Present (VI) and the Future (VII).

Of the minor arcana, the cards in positions 7 to 12 indicate the Future, those in positions 1 to 4 indicate the Past and those in positions 4 to 7 indicate the Present.

The above figures indicate the numbers of the positions to be occupied by the cards. It is important to take note of this so as to avoid making the mistake of thinking that arcanum VII must always be in position VII. But in any case my readers are sufficiently intelligent that I need say no more.

Explaining the meanings of the cards will present no problems once you have read lessons 2 and 3. Besides, practice will teach you all the details better than all the theories in the world.

THE TAROT—HOW TO USE THE TAROT TO OBTAIN ORACLES

I have borrowed the following study from the excellent work *Le Tarot*, by Mr. Bourgeat.

I—THE DOVE

Take from the deck the same number of cards as the Christian name by which the beloved is usually known. Then go through the deck and find the querent card (arcanum XXII) plus the card intended to represent the beloved (Page, Queen or King). Add these cards to the ones already drawn and lay the set of cards in a semi-circle face downwards.

Then, slowly, pick up the cards one by one at random and still proceeding at a very slow pace, place them in a semi-circle—from left to right—turning them over as you go.

When the interpretation is finished, pick up the cards, shuffle them and put them into three piles:

the first for the querent or the heart of the querent;
the second for heart of the beloved;
the third for unforeseen matters.

II—The Hawk

The procedure is exactly the same, but instead of being about the object of the querent's affections it concerns an enemy.

You end up with the following three piles:
the first for the querent;
the second for the enemy;
the third for unforeseen matters.

III—The Pearls of Isis

Take seven cards from the deck and place seven more over them so as to form crosses. Interpret these cards one by one.

The Gypsy Method, as taken from a Catalan grimoire

Take the whole deck, shuffle it well and make twelve piles of four cards.

Take the first pile as relating to all matters concerning the life of the person concerned: their constitution, their temperament, their body, their habits and their lifespan.
The second pile relates to their degree of wealth or poverty and their possessions, and to trade or business matters.
The third pile relates to their family, both blood relations and relations by marriage.
The fourth pile relates to property, inheritance, hidden treasures and hoped-for benefits.
The fifth pile relates to love, pregnancy, births, the sex and number of children, romantic liaisons and domestic ups and downs.
The sixth pile relates to illnesses and their cause and treatment, and to recovery from illness.
The seventh pile relates to marriage and enmities.
The eighth pile relates to death.
The ninth pile relates to sciences, arts, employment and the different professions.

The tenth pile relates to all things connected with government and the administration of the State.

The eleventh pile relates to friendship, charity and generous sentiments.

The twelfth pile relates to pain and sorrow and to persecution of all kinds.

It is not enough to use one pile in order to resolve a matter. You need to take at least three piles and form a trigon. The trigons consist of four cards each, as follows:

```
1     5     9
2     6    10
3     7    11
4     8    12
```

For example, suppose the question is whether a given person is loved by another given person. This is a question belonging to the fifth pile, so take the pile in question and place the four cards in a row. Then take the ninth pile and place the cards underneath. Lastly, take the first pile and place the cards underneath the previous ones to form a third row.

All that remains now is the interpretation.

(This Gypsy method is an adaptation of the astrological houses to Tarot—**PAPUS**).

Interpretations of the Thirty-Two Cards
(according to the famous Moreau)

The Kings

King of Coins: soldier; reversed, male country dweller;
King of Cups: blond businessman; reversed, man of heart;
King of Swords: member of the legal profession; reversed, bad man;
King of Wands: dark man, fidelity; reversed, human sickness.

The Queens

Queen of Coins: traitress; reversed, country woman;
Queen of Cups: good fair-haired woman; reversed, good woman;
Queen of Swords: widow; reversed, bad woman;
Queen of Wands: Loving Woman; reversed, indecision.

The Pages

Page of Coins: traitor; reversed: servant;
Page of Cups: young fair-haired man; reversed: thoughts of the fair-haired man;
Page of Swords: traitor; reversed: illness;
Page of Wands: faithful man; reversed: indecision.

The Aces

Ace of Coins: great news; reversed: letter or note;
Ace of Cups: House of the True Heart; reversed: House of the False Heart;
Ace of Swords: trial, pregnancy; reversed: letter, trifle;
Ace of Wands: money; reversed: love.

The Tens

Ten of Coins: decisive campaign; reversed: delay;
Ten of Cups: wholehearted rest; reversed: Repose of the False heart;

Ten of Swords: boredom; reversed: tears;
Ten of Wands: good fortune; reversed: love.

THE NINES

Nine of Coins: route, journey; reversed: delay;
Nine of Cups: victory or gift; reversed: great victory;
Nine of Swords: death; reversed: prison;
Nine of Wands: money; reversed: wheel of fortune.

THE EIGHTS

Eight of Coins: taking a step; reversed: same meaning;
Eight of Cups: young fair-haired woman; reversed: great joy;
Eight of Swords: intense sorrow; reversed: worries;
Eight of Wands: declaration of love; reversed: jealousy.

THE SEVENS

Seven of Coins: quarrel; reversed: snub or humiliation;
Seven of Cups: fair-haired child; reversed: child;
Seven of Swords: young dark-haired woman; reversed: snub or humiliation;
Seven of Wands: dark-haired child; reversed : bastard.

Drawing the Cards in Fifteens

I shall start by describing the French way of drawing the cards in fifteens, since this is the most commonly-used method.

Take a deck of 32 cards, shuffle them thoroughly and cut them yourself if you are using the cards on your own behalf, or else ask the querent to cut them with their left hand. Then make two piles of 16 cards each, choose or ask the querent to choose one of these piles and put the bottom card to one side as the surprise card. Lay the other 15 cards out in front of you from left to right, and look and see if the person representing the querent is among them. If not, then you must shuffle the 32 cards again and keep repeating the process until the querent card appears in the chosen stack.

For example, let us suppose that, when the cards are drawn after having been shuffled and cut, the following cards appear in the querent's chosen pile: Ace of Hearts, nine of Clubs, King of Hearts, ten of Diamonds, nine of Hearts, eight of Hearts, Ace of Diamonds, Jack of Diamonds, Queen of Spades, Ace of Clubs, nine of Diamonds, seven of Diamonds and seven of Hearts, plus the eight of Clubs as the card in reserve.

Now here is the interpretation of the 15 cards. The Ace of Hearts is followed by the nine of Clubs, the King of Hearts, the ten of Diamonds, the nine of Hearts, the eight of Hearts and the Ace of Diamonds. Therefore, these seven cards denote profit, great commercial success and satisfactory solutions. The eight cards that follow on from these, the Jack of Diamonds, Queen of Spades, Ace of Clubs, nine of Diamonds, the seven of Clubs, the seven of Hearts and the surprise card, the eight of Clubs indicate a soldier's surprise, a campaign and something of great advantage to whoever is concerned. This is the first interpretation.

Now reshuffle the 15 cards, ask the querent to cut them, and then divide them into three piles, still putting one card aside. This process is to be repeated three times. Note that, for this purpose, you always take the first card or the last one and place it with the card you have set aside as the surprise card. Next ask the querent to choose one pile for himself or herself, one pile for the house and one pile for the unexpected. Then take each pile one after the other and interpret it according to the individual meanings of the cards and the way in which the cards relate to one another, ending with the surprise pile.

Drawing the Cards in Twenty Ones

Shuffle the 32 cards and discard the first 11, then lay the remaining 21 cards out from left to right. If the querent is among these 21 cards, interpret them. If not, start again as indicated in the method for the 15 card spread. The procedure is much the same, the only difference being that the three piles: the querent; his/her house; the unexpected consist of six cards each and the surprise pile consists of only three cards.

Drawing the Cards in Threes

Shuffle the cards thoroughly and ask the querent to cut them with the left hand. Then turn the cards face upwards three at a time. Whenever two cards of the same suit appear in a set of three, put the stronger of the two aside. If you happen to get three cards of the same suit or of the same value, for example, three Kings, three Queens, three Aces etc., put all three of them aside. Shuffle the remaining cards again, get the querent to cut them and start drawing them in threes once again. Continue with this process until 15 cards have been put to one side including the querent card, for if this card were not present, you would need to keep repeating the process until it did appear. After this, continue as per the instructions given above for drawing cards by 15s.

Drawing the Cards in Sevens

The method for drawing cards in 7s differs little from that for drawing cards in 3s. Once the cards have been shuffled and cut, discard the first six and then put the 7th to one side. Continue this process until you reach the end of the deck, and then repeat three times, so that you end up with twelve cards. If the querent is not among these twelve cards the whole operation must be repeated. The method of interpreting the relationships between the cards is the same as usual.

184 THE DIVINATORY TAROT

Drawing the Cards in Twenty Twos or the Great Star Spread

Let us suppose the querent is a blond-haired man, and therefore represented by the King of Hearts. First take this card and lay it on the table face upwards. Then shuffle the remaining 31 cards and ask the querent to cut them. Discard the first ten cards and place the eleventh card on its side underneath the King of Hearts. Cut the cards again and place the top card above the querent card (in this case the King of Hearts). Keep repeating this process, placing the cards in the sequence shown by the figures in the table opposite[1].

In the table as illustrated the 21 cards surrounding the King of Hearts: Ace of Spades; Ace of Clubs; Ace of Diamonds; eight of Hearts; Jack of Hearts; Queen of Spades; Queen of Clubs; eight of Spades; Jack of Diamonds; ten of Diamonds; seven of Hearts; seven of Clubs; ten of Clubs; nine of Spades; eight of Diamonds; Jack of Spades; King of Spades; seven of Spades; ten of Hearts and seven of Diamonds. Now take the cards in succession as follows.

In order to read the cards, start with the longest radius. In other words, join card number 16, in this case the 8 of Diamonds with card no. 14, the 9 of Spades. Read the individual meanings of the two cards, draw out the interpretation and continue to explain the cards with the longest radii two by two. Then go on to explain those cards forming the second longest radii, always progressing from left to right, thus, 10 of Diamonds with Queen of Spades and so on. The same procedure applies when explaining the four cards that form the central radii: Ace of Diamonds with 8 of Hearts and Ace of Spades with Ace of Clubs.

One last card remains to be read, and it is the seven of diamonds, positioned underneath the King of Hearts. Interpret it according to what it said above in the table giving the meanings of the individual cards.

---

[1] This table does not appear in any of the French versions.

The Italian Method

The Italian method is the least used method of all. Nonetheless, to the true cartomancer it is indispensable. Those who consult the cards purely as a pastime can dispense with the necessity of practising it. But no-one working purely in the interest of science must omit anything that might enlighten them further. The Italian method does not actually differ greatly from the French one. The only real difference is the way in which you obtain the cards for interpretation purposes. Here are the procedures.

Shuffle the cards, and then cut them if doing a reading for yourself, or else ask the querent to cut them. Here too, always cut with the left hand.

Turn the cards over three at a time, and each time two cards of the same suit appear among the group of three put the stronger of them to one side. If all three cards are of the same suit, put all of them to one side. If they are all of different suits put none of them aside. Shuffle the cards again, apart from the ones that have been put to one side. Cut them or ask the querent to cut them, and recommence the process of drawing them in threes until you are left with 15 cards. These must include the querent card. If the querent card is not present, you need to repeat the procedure until it does appear. Then lay the resulting 15 cards out from left to right, face upwards, and examine them as a group. Let us suppose the querent is a fair-haired woman represented by the Queen of Hearts, and that the 15 cards are arranged as follows:

> Ace of diamonds
> Eight of Hearts
> Ace of Spades
> Queen of Clubs
> Eight of Spades
> Queen of Hearts
> Jack of Diamonds
> Eight of Diamonds
>
> Seven of Clubs
> King of Hearts
> Nine of Spades
> Seven of Hearts
> Eight of Diamonds
> Ten of Clubs
> Seven of Spades

Having examined all the cards you will notice that there are two Aces. Explain the meaning of these on the basis of the interpretation

I taught earlier. Do the same with the two Queens, the two Tens, the three Eights and the three Sevens.

Then count out one for the Queen of Hearts, which represents the female querent, two for the Jack of Diamonds, three for the Ten of Diamonds, four for the Seven of Clubs and five for the King of Hearts. Stop there and explain the combination as set out in the French method. Start again, and count one for the King of Hearts, which is the point at which you stopped before, then count up to five, which takes you to the Ten of Clubs. Keep counting the cards in fives and reading the fifth card until the fifth card turns out to be the male querent card. Then take the cards two by two, one from the right and one from the left, and explain them as per the French method.

Shuffle the cards, ask the querent to cut them, then arrange them into five stacks, face downwards, placing one card on the first stack, which represents the male querent, one card in the second stack, which represents the house, one card in the third stack, which represents the expected, one card in the fourth pack, which represents the unexpected and one card in the fifth stack, which is the surprise. Keep going until you reach the last card, and put this to one side as what is known as the consolation card. The surprise packet will consist of two cards only, whereas the four other stacks will contain three. Turn the stacks over one by one starting with the first stack, and explain them according to the interpretations I taught previously.

General Observations

Since it would be impossible to give solutions for each change of cards, you simply need to gain a good knowledge of the meanings of the 32 cards as discussed above, and pay attention to the methods described in this work for drawing cards in sevens, fifteens and twenty-ones or according to any other method, and in this way you can be your own oracle.

If the four Aces and the four Tens appear in a spread this means great profit and gain for the querent: a prize or an inheritance. The four Kings indicate great success and the four Queens indicate a great deal of gossip about the querent, whereas the four Jacks signify disputes and fights.

It is also important to point out that, when drawing the cards in fifteens or twenty-ones, if the majority are minor arcana then this indicates great success for the person concerned. If the five lowest Spades are present then the querent will learn of the death of a relative or friend. If the five lowest Clubs are present then this indicates success in winning a legal case or in other matters. If the five lowest Diamonds and Hearts are present, then there will be good news of military campaigns and of all good-hearted persons involved, provided the querent is a good person.

If the question is about the separation of persons and goods, you need to draw twenty-one cards. If the four nines are present separation is guaranteed, but if the four Queens are there, separation will never take place.

If a cause for jealousy is well founded, the fifteen card spread will include five Diamonds. If it is not well founded there will be five Hearts plus the Seven of Clubs.

In the case of an enterprise of any kind, in order to denote success, there need to be four Aces plus the nine of Hearts in the spread. If the nine of Spades appears before the querent, the enterprise will not be successful.

In the case of a game of chance, a twenty-one card spread is needed, and it must contain the eight Clubs, the four Aces and the four Kings if the querent is to win.

If you want to know whether a child will make good and whether he will keep his inheritance, the presence of the four Aces will guarantee both this and a suitable love match. If the child is a girl, the cards you need are the four eights plus the King of Hearts, and these are an omen of peace and harmony within her household.

In order to know how long it will be in years, months or weeks before a couple gets married, if it is a matter of years, the King of Spades will appear along with the Queen of Hearts, the Ace of Spades and the eight of Diamonds. Any other eights will indicate as many years' delay, any other nine as many months' delay and any other seven as many weeks' delay.

If a man is to carve out a successful military career for himself there need to be four Kings together with the four tens, and if the four Aces happen to be there too, then he will reach the highest rank of which he is capable. In the case of a change of property or place the cards depend upon whether the person involved is master, mistress or servant. In the case of a master or mistress there need to be four Jacks, the ten and the eight of Diamonds and the ten of Clubs in order for matters to reach a successful conclusion. If the 9 of Diamonds is present it means there will be a delay. In the case of a servant the ten and seven of Diamonds, the eight of Spades and the four Queens need to be present if matters are to reach a successful conclusion.

Original Method of Drawing Tarot Cards by Etteilla
(according to one of his rarest works)

I have just set out a method that is for the most part personal. So since it has never been my intention to monopolise the art of cartomancy, I am going to say a bit about a method used by the master of this field of occultism, namely Etteilla.

Etteilla's real name was Aliette. He lived during the era of the French Revolution, and began his working life as a hairdresser. He came across a Tarot deck quite by chance, and intrigued by its strangeness, began to study it. He continued to study it for thirty years, by which time he believed he had discovered the secrets of this Ancient Egyptian book. Unfortunately, Etteilla had no synthetic material to go by, and this led him to put down some sadly delusional thoughts along with the truly wonderful intuitive insights. People are too quick to slander this tireless worker. We should recognise the real truths contained in his work and not pay too much attention to the naivety that mars it in places. In any case, Etteilla applied his knowledge to fortune telling, and if his contemporaries are to be believed, he was amazingly good at it. Thus he became God in the eyes of the female cartomancers who came after him and who now swear by him alone.

That is why I shall confine myself to setting out his method in detail. I feel there is no point in talking about those of his female successors, who merely stepped into his shoes without understanding him.

There are four stages to drawing the cards according to this method, and I shall set them out one by one.

Stage One—Shuffle the whole Tarot deck, both major and minor arcana, then cut the cards and divide them into three stacks of 26 cards each (1) as follows:

26   26   26

Take the middle stack and put it to one side on your right as follows:

$$26 \qquad 26 \qquad 26 \text{ set aside}$$

You are now left with two stacks of 26 cards. Take these, shuffle them, cut them and divide them into three stacks of 17 cards each.

$$17 \qquad 17 \qquad 17$$
$$1$$

You are left with one card, which you can disregard from now on. Take the middle stack and place in to your right next to the stack of 26 cards you have already set aside, as follows:

$$17 \qquad 17 \qquad 17 \qquad 26 \text{ set aside}$$
$$1$$

Etteilla understood perfectly that the number 26 corresponded to the divine name [yod heh vau heh], the sum of which gives

$$10 + \ 5 + \ 6 + \ 5 = 26$$
$$\text{yod} \quad \text{heh} \quad \text{vau} \quad \text{heh}$$

Now take the 35 cards that are not set aside, shuffle them thoroughly, cut them or get the querent to cut them and divide them into three stacks of 11 cards each as follows:

$$11 \qquad 11 \qquad 11$$
$$2$$

Two cards remain and you can disregard those. As before, take the middle stack and place it to your right next to the two others that are already there, as follows:

$$11 \quad 11 \quad 11 \quad 17 \quad 26$$
$$2$$

Having done this, put all the cards you have not put aside into one stack. You are now ready to read the oracles.

First of all take the stack of 26 cards you have set to one side and lay it out on the table card by card from right to left as follows:

26 through to 1

Take the stack of 17 cards and lay it out in the same way underneath the first stack, then lay out the stack of 11 cards underneath the other two stacks. You will end up with the following arrangement:

Heart	26 through to 1
Mind	17 through to 1
Body	11 through to 1
Reject Stack 24	

Now explain the meanings of the cards, bearing in mind that the bottom stack of 11 cards is about the querent's body, the middle stack of 17 cards is about their mind and the top stack is to do with their heart.

From this method of drawing the cards Etteilla made some subtle deductions about the creation of the world, the Kabbalah and the Philosopher's Stone. There is no point in dwelling on these for the moment. Instead let us continue to study his methods of drawing the cards.

Stage Two—Shuffle all 78 of the cards again and cut them or get the querent to cut them. Then take the first 17 cards from the card and arrange them thus:

17 through to 1

Take a good look at the eighteenth card (the one that comes to hand after you have laid out the first seventeen) and the seventy-eighth card, which will be at the bottom of the deck. The meaning of these two cards will tell you whether or not a good flow of friendly communication has been established between you and the querent.

You can now read the oracles formed by the above line, starting on the right as usual. When you have read the line, put the seventeenth

DRAWING AND READING TAROT CARDS

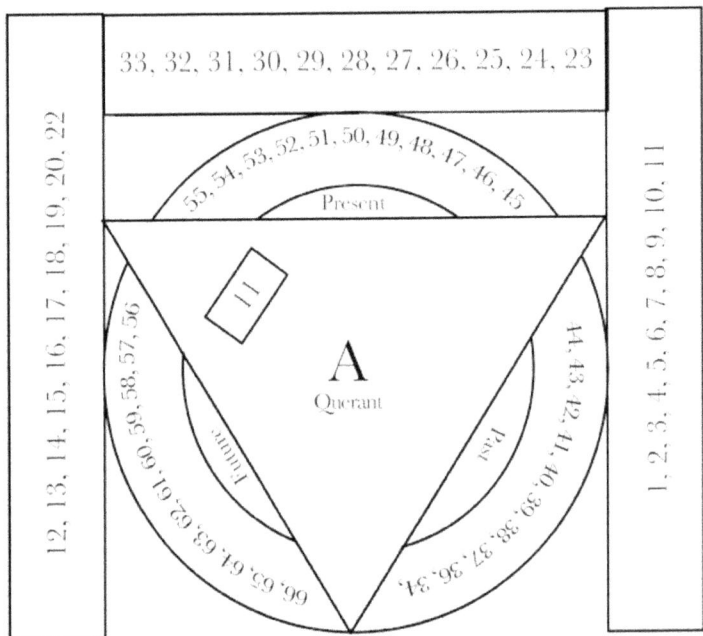

card on one side to the right of you and the first card to the left of you, then the sixteenth and the second and so on until there is just one card left in the middle. This card goes to one side[1].

Stage Three—Take all your cards, shuffle them and cut them or ask the querent to cut them. Then arrange them as shown in the following diagram and according to the numbering given.

This gives you Etteilla's major configuration, which provides the key to the past, present and future of the person consulting the cards. Therefore, in order to make fruitful use of this method you need to memorise this figure and keep it in mind at all times. The best thing to do is draw it on a table or a large sheet of paper, including all the numbers, then arrange the cards according in the correct numerical positions.

---

[1] Perhaps I have failed to understand Etteilla clearly—his books, Which I am trying to make understandable, were in fact extremely obscure—but this last exercise seems completely pointless.

In order to read the results of this configuration you need to take the cards in twos: the 1st together with the 34th, the 2nd with the 35th, etc. for the past.

The 3rd with the 43rd, the 24th with the 46th…the 33rd with the 55th for the present.

The 12th with the 66th, the 13th with the 65th…the 22nd with the 56th for the future.

Studying the table will enable you to achieve a perfect understanding of all that.

Stage Four – The fourth stage is now merely secondary. It serves to obtain answers to whatever questions a person might want to ask. In order to arrive at it you shuffle all the cards, cut them or get the querent to cut them, then draw the top seven from the deck as follows:

7 through to 1

and read the response.

And that is how you draw the cards according to Etteilla's own original method. What I have given in these few pages is a summary of one of Etteilla's works, a pamphlet called *The Book of Thoth*. An obscure work from a number of points of view, it also contains a portrait of Etteilla. Like all the author's works it is extremely rare. Let me add that not one of Etteilla's numerous followers made a serious attempt at elucidating his work. I believe I am one of the first to set it out according to such simple principles.

In Chapter 7 you will find a supplement to this method together with further explanations.

CHAPTER FOUR

Interplay of the cards

Reading the teachings of the Tarot card by card is like playing the piano note by note with one finger. It lacks accompaniment and harmony. The art of true Tarot reading lies in knowledge of the interaction between the cards, in other words, the way in which the cards influence one another. It is precisely the knowledge of interplay that distinguishes the older cartomancer who has been working with the cards for many years from the young inexperienced reader who does the cards for her own amusement.

The interaction between two, three or four cards from the four suits can result in several tens of thousands of meanings. Clearly, I cannot give all these meanings. Most of all I wish to keep things clear and provide practical tuition, so I shall only quote the most frequently occurring instances.

In former times, it was common practice to combine the science of interaction between the cards with that of numbers. For example, the interplay between the 10th major arcanum, the 10 of Wands and the Knight of Cups would give:

10. The number of the major arcanum;
26. The number of the 10 of Wands according to Etteilla;
38. The number of the Knight of Cups.

A total of 74. If you add the 7 and the 4 together you get 11, the number of the arcana representing moral strength, and this is the meaning of the interplay.

The Meanings of Two Cards Positioned Side by Side within the Spread
(The cards marked with asterisks are reversed)

The Ace and ten of Cups mean a surprise event in the home.
Seven of Cups and seven of Wands – Thoughts of money.
Seven of Cups and ten of Coins – You will receive gold.
Ten of Wands and ten of Swords** - Loss of money.
Ten of Swords and ten of Wands** - Money in the evening.
Eight of Coins and Ace of Wands* - Gift of gold.
Ace of Cups and Page of Coins – Someone is waiting for you with anticipation.
Page of Cups and Ace of Swords* - Worries about a political matter.
Ace of Swords and seven of Swords* - Trial.
Page of Swords and Ace of Swords – Second Marriage.
Queen of Swords and eight of Cups – a fair-haired widow.
Ace of Wands and seven of Cups* - Large amounts of money.
Page of Coins and seven of Swords – You await something.
Queen of Coins* and King of Coins – Male stranger.
Queen of Swords* and Queen of Wands – Injustice.
King of Cups* and Ace of Cups – Ballroom.
Ace of Wands close to the ten of Wands – A sum of money.
King of Cups* and Ace of Cups* - Moneylenders.
Seven of Coins and Queen of Coins** - Quarrel or dispute.

Queen of Cups* and King of Coins – Obstacle to a marriage.
King and nine of Swords** - Unjust accusation.
King and Queen of Cups – Respectable elderly persons.
Eight and Ace of Wands – Declaration of love.
Page and Queen of Coins – Female servant.
Ten of Coins and eight of Cups* - Unexpected journey.
King and Ace of Cups** - Stock exchange.
King and Queen of Wands – Married couple.
Seven of Cups and ten of Swords* - Loss of a small item.
Ten of Swords and seven of Cups* - Surprise, astonishment.
Queen of Wands and seven of Coins* - Discussion.
Eight of Coins and eight of Wands – Faraway campaign.
Ten of Swords and card no. 1 – Jealous tears.
Eight of Coins and eight of Swords – Serious illness.
Ace of Wands* and ten of Swords – Jealousy in love.
Eight of Coins and seven of Swords* - Indecisive stage of campaign.
Ace of Cups and ten of Coins – A shock or blow.
King* and Ace of Cups – Game of chance.
Ace of Wands* and ten of Cups – Surprise in love.
Seven of Swords and Ace of Wands* - Gift made in friendship.
Ace of Cups and seven of Coins – Domestic proposals.
Eight of Coins and seven of Cups* - Planned moves.
Ten of Wands and ten of Cups – Surprise in the form of money.

Individual Meanings of the Thirty-two Cards

The Kings

Coins: friendship, marriage; reversed, many problems will occur.
Cups: accountable man willing to oblige you; reversed, the opposite.
Swords: lawyer with whom you will do business; reversed, failed legal proceedings, business upset.
Wands: just, fair-minded person who will protect you; reversed, bad luck, uncertainty of success.

The Queens

Coins: fair-haired countrywoman who indulges in scandal-mongering at the querent's expense; reversed, covetousness, wrongs.
Cups: honest, devoted woman who will do you a service; obstacle to marriage depending on the female querent.
Swords: distressed woman, widow or woman with money problems; reversed, major business problems; if the querent is a young woman, she is betrayed by the man she loves.
Wands: dark-haired female rival; alongside a man, fidelity, preference for the one she is with; if near another queen, she is interested in the querent; reversed, desire, jealousy, infidelity.

The Pages

Coins: soldier, postman or postilion bringing news; reversed, unfavourable news in connection with the subject matter of the consultation.
Cups: soldier soon to appear before, or young man inclined to do great service and with whom the querent will be connected. It has the same meaning both on the right and on the left.
Swords: unprincipled ne'er-do-well; man with no finesse deriding the most sacred things; reversed, the same person concerned with overcoming obstacles to his plans.
Wands: a lover, a well-bred young man looking for a young woman: next to a queen it denotes success; next to a man, someone who will

speak on his behalf; followed by the Page of Cups, a rival who is a threat; reversed, the young man's parents will oppose the marriage.

THE ACES

Ace of Coins: letters and news imminent with the aid of the mark indicating the top of the card; reversed, sad news.

Ace of Cups: Joy, contentment; accompanied by face cards, feasts, libations; reversed, the pleasures to come will be tempered by sorrows.

Ace of Swords: Advantages gained by force, conquest, success in love, violent passion; reversed, same meaning; also disastrous result or everything turns to your disadvantage. If followed by the ten and the nine this denotes news of a death, great sorrow, betrayal be persons close to you or even theft.

Ace of Wands: letter announcing the arrival of money, good fortune in the near future, inheritance, success or financial dealings; reversed, joy tempered by a few dark clouds, if followed by the Ace of Coins or the seven of Wands, gain, profit, great success in business, money coming in, commercial prosperity.

THE TENS

Ten of Coins: great joy, change of location and area.

Ten of Cups: joy, contentment: if surrounded by several face cards it represents someone who will act in your interests.

Ten of Swords: if followed by the Ace and the King it means prison; for a woman or girl it means betrayal by friends.

Ten of Wands: gain, prosperity, success in all matters, but if followed by the nine of Swords these are cancelled out; if legal proceedings are involved the case will definitely be lost.

THE NINES*

Nine of Coins: a minor delay, but this will not disrupt the querent's affairs.

---

* The 9 of Wands is missing in the original version

Nine of Cups: harmony and contentment for those for whom you have drawn the cards.

Nine of Swords: delay and failure in some affairs; if followed by the nine of Coins or the Ace of Wands you will receive money but after some delay.

The Eights

Eight of Coins: a young man from the world of commerce who will take steps on behalf of the querent.

Eight of Cups: if the querent is married their children will instinctively incline towards good actions in all things; if the querent is single, they will be completely successful in all matters.

Eight of Swords: if followed by the seven of Coins it means that someone will be the bearer of bad news, if next to any face card it means tears, discord and loss of job or reputation for the querent.

Eight of Wands: means moves in connection with money or business, high hopes, good fortune guaranteed.

The Sevens

Seven of Coins: means good news, particularly if it is near the nine of Wands and the Ace of Coins; great success in games of chance.

Seven of Cups: if the querent is a young single woman, then she will have daughters after she marries; if the querent is a young single man, he will marry a worthy young woman.

Seven of Swords: means quarrels and torment for the person represented by the card that follows, unless it is side by side with several Cups, in which case this means security, independence and relief from troubles.

Seven of Wands: heralds weakness in love affecting the querent; however, if followed by the seven of Coins and the nine of Wands, it denotes abundance of goods and an inheritance from distant relatives.

Where several cards of the same value appear together, for example, 2, 3, or 4 Kings, Queens or Pages etc., Etteilla attributes the following meanings to them.

Looking at the cards on your right hand side

4 Kings. Great honours;
3 Kings. Consultation;
2 Kings. Small piece of advice;

4 Queens. Major negotiations;
3 Queens. Betrayal by women;
2 Queens. Woman friend;

4 Pages. Infectious illness;
3 Pages. Dispute;
2 Pages. Worry;

4 Aces. Game of chance;
3 Aces. Minor success;
2 Aces. Trickery;

4 Tens. Habitual criminal;
3 Tens. Change in condition;
2 Tens. Change;

4 Nines. Good citizen;
3 Nines. Great success;
2 Nines. Small sum of money;

4 Eights. Setback;
3 Eights. Marriage;
2 Eights. New acquaintance;

4 Sevens. Intrigue;
3 Sevens. Infirmity;
2 Sevens. Trivial piece of news.

Looking at the cards on your left hand side

4.Kings. Celerity;
3 Kings. Commerce;
2 Kings. Plan;

4 Queens. Bad company;
3 Queens. Gourmandise;
2 Queens. Company;

4 Pages. Privation;
3 Pages. Indolence;
2 Pages. Worker, work;

4 Aces. Dishonour;
3 Aces. Debauchery;
2 Aces. Enemy;

4 Tens. Event;
3 Tens. Lack;
2 Tens. Waiting;

4 Nines. Usury;
3 Nines. Imprudence;
2 Nines. Profit;

4 Eights. Error;
3 Eights. Spectacle;
2 Eights. Hitch;

4 Sevens. Bad citizen;
3 Sevens. Joy;
2 Sevens. Prostitute.

Three Kings

1. King of Cups
2. King of Coins
3. King of Wands

The person will progress from a state of misfortune to one of extreme good fortune and happiness. They will possess worldly goods and immense wealth, and honours will be bestowed upon them.

1. King of Cups
2. King of Coins
3. King of Swords

The person will make no headway in acquiring greater fortune than they already possess despite all their efforts.

1. King of Cups
2. King of Wands
3. King of Coins

The person's circumstances will change on account of their own abilities, and they will prosper, gaining both honours and riches in the process.

1. King of Cups
2. King of Wands
3. King of Swords

The person's inheritance will make them wealthy, and it will be within their scope to make some fortunate…**

1. King of Cups
2. King of Swords
3. King of Wands

The death of a child will change the person's circumstances on account of the property they receive as a result.

1. King of Cups
2. King of Swords
3. King of Coins

The person will be betrayed by their own friends, and this will destroy all their hopes when they least expect it and upset their fortunes greatly.

1. King of Wands
2. King of Coins
3. King of Cups

The person will be given back some stolen family property, and this action will alter their circumstances and bring them considerable wealth.

1. King of Wands
2. King of Coins
3. King of Swords

** This sentence seems incomplete in the original French

The person will be obliged to give back an item of property which has been to their benefit, but which does not belong to them, and this will disrupt their circumstances a great deal.

1. King of Wands
2. King of Swords
3. King of Cups

The person will find a hidden treasure, and this will bring them wealth and happiness for the rest of their life.

1. King of Wands
2. King of Swords
3. King of Coins

The person will lose some items of property in a fire, and this will alter their circumstances for a while. But with patience and hard work they will become as wealthy as before.

1. King of Wands
2. King of Cups
3. King of Coins

The person will rise above their station and alter their circumstances as a result of well-deserved favours. The rewards they receive will attract no end of envy on the part of others.

1. King of Wands
2. King of Cups
3. King of Swords

The person is born to be esteemed by faithful friends and benefactors, who will procure them a happy marriage.

1. King of Coins
2. King of Cups
3. King of Wands

With the aid of kind relatives or good deeds on the part of several friends, the person will rise to a state in which they acquire both honour and wealth.

1. King of Coins
2. King of Cups
3. King of Swords

The person will have a major win in a game of chance.

1. King of Coins
2. King of Wands
3. King of Cups

The person will have the opportunity to be of considerable service to a great personage. The latter will show appreciation by providing them with a means of claiming protection through a service that will ensure them good fortune for the rest of their life.

The person will prosper with the help of relatives or friend.

1. King of Coins
2. King of Swords
3. King of Cups

The person will fall into disfavour for having spoken out too much against a great personage at a meeting.

1. King of Coins
2. King of Swords
3. King of Wands

Having entrusted their affairs too much to others, the person will consequently not benefit from them, but will suffer mortification as a result of envy and betrayal.

1. King of Swords
2. King of Cups
3. King of Wands

The person will handle an affair of the heart in which both honour and interests are at stake, and with the help of friends the outcome will be successful.

1. King of Swords
2. King of Cups
3. King of Coins

The person will find both their person and their property under attack. A courageous and kind man will fend off the attacks and deliver the person from unfortunate events.

1. King of Swords
2. King of Wands
3. King of Cups

The person will receive a gift of some consequence, given by relatives or benefactors as a token of gratitude for their constancy.

1. King of Swords
2. King of Wands
3. King of Coins

The person will acquire a friend in whom they will place all their confidence, and about whom they will have no suspicions whatsoever. The friend will steal their jewellery and their money.

1. King of Swords
2. King of Coins
3. King of Cups

The person will triumph over two of their enemies through wise advice, and this will make them revered in the minds of decent citizens on account of the modesty that accompanies these victorious acts.

1. King of Swords
2. King of Coins
3. King of Wands

The person will suffer stomach ailments caused by water.

All the explanations for the interaction between these Kings applies regardless of the places or numbers where the three Kings occur. The same applies to the other card combinations.

THREE QUEENS

1. Queen of Cups
2. Queen of Coins
3. Queen of Wands

The person will always be happy on account of the initiatives of close relatives with regard to their household affairs.

1. Queen of Cups
2. Queen of Coins
3. Queen of Swords

The person will be ill rewarded by relatives and, furthermore, would be well advised not to ask them for any money.

1. Queen of Cups
2. Queen of Wands
3. Queen of Coins

The person will enjoy all the support imaginable from close relatives. They will be loved and cherished.

1. Queen of Cups
2. Queen of Wands
3. Queen of Swords

The person will be well loved by their relations by marriage, such as brother-in-law, daughter-in-law, nieces and nephews. They will receive all manner of possessions in the future.

1. Queen of Cups
2. Queen of Swords
3. Queen of Wands

Meeting of relatives or close friends to conclude an affair which will be to the person's advantage, and which will bring them guaranteed prosperity.

1. Queen of Cups
2. Queen of Swords
3. Queen of Coins

Meeting of false-hearted relatives or friends for purposes detrimental to the person's future well-being, and during which they will plot to destroy a transaction that would have secured the person's lifelong good fortune. The person will become aware of this six months later.

1. Queen of Wands
2. Queen of Coins
3. Queen of Cups

The kindness and attention of the person towards a rich elderly person will be extremely well rewarded.

1. Queen of Wands
2. Queen of Coins
3. Queen of Swords

The person will neglect a long-standing relative or friend out of pride or unkindness, thus doing them considerable wrong.

1. Queen of Wands
2. Queen of Swords
3. Queen of Cups

A friend will leave the person all their worldly goods in a will or as a gift.

1. Queen of Wands
2. Queen of Swords
3. Queen of Coins

A meeting of false friends will be disastrous to the person's fortunes. But after two years, their troubles will begin to pass, and their circumstances will keep on improving steadily until the day they die.

1. Queen of Wands
2. Queen of Cups
3. Queen of Coins

For the good of the person concerned there will be a meeting of relatives, friends and superiors, who will make a decision to the person's advantage. The latter will derive honour and profit from it.

1. Queen of Wands
2. Queen of Cups
3. Queen of Swords

The person will form a close bond with someone during the course of a gathering. The other person will become so attached to them that the union will become a source of permanent happiness.

1. Queen of Coins
2. Queen of Cups
3. Queen of Wands

The person's own wit will earn them the esteem and affection of people who will make them happy.

1. Queen of Coins
2. Queen of Cups
3. Queen of Swords

The person will find a sum of money in a hidden place, and this will make their fortune.

1. Queen of Coins
2. Queen of Wands
3. Queen of Cups

Through the advice of a friend and through their own taste for knowledge, the person will emerge from the confines they had set themselves. Then through a combination of work and circumstances, they will obtain a well-deserved prize that will go on to earn them their fortune.

1. Queen of Coins
2. Queen of Wands
3. Queen of Swords

On account of their own stubbornness, the person will lose two friends, who will then hinder their progress with an initiative that would otherwise have succeeded.

1. Queen of Coins
2. Queen of Swords
3. Queen of Cups

Excessive weakness and belief in a false friend will cause the person to follow the friend's ideas too slavishly, thus arousing contempt for them in the minds of right-thinking citizens.

1. Queen of Coins
2. Queen of Swords
3. Queen of Wands

The person will abandon the path of justice and create bad fortune for others.

1. Queen of Swords
2. Queen of Cups
3. Queen of Wands

Out of pure friendship, true friends will make sure that the person succeeds in all reasonable enterprises.

1. Queen of Swords
2. Queen of Cups
3. Queen of Coins

The person will be indifferent to the wise advice of others, and will consequently make considerable errors, which will cause them a great deal of regret.

1. Queen of Swords
2. Queen of Wands
3. Queen of Cups

The person will win the friendship of virtuous persons on their own merit, and this will bring them happiness.

1. Queen of Swords
2. Queen of Wands
3. Queen of Coins

The person will cause others to suspect their integrity and virtue on account of negligence in their own affairs.

1. Queen of Swords
2. Queen of Coins
3. Queen of Cups

Bored with their state of well-being, the person's turbulent spirit will cause them to suffer humiliation, and in turn people will cease to respect them for a few years. But they will change their ways, thus regaining public support, and this will enable them to recover their lost fortune.

1. Queen of Swords
2. Queen of Coins
3. Queen of Wands

The person commits the fault of loving without being loved, and the only way they will find help is through their own strength of mind.

THREE PAGES

1. Page of Cups
2. Page of Coins
3. Page of Wands

Despite contemptible manoeuvres on the part of an enemy, the person will win a case on which their permanent good fortune depends.

1. Page of Cups
2. Page of Wands
3. Page of Coins

The person will sort out some affairs of great consequence in spite of envy on the part of friends or relatives. Once concluded, these affairs will cause things to go smoothly for him and enable him to lead a pleasant life.

1. Page of Cups
2. Page of Wands
3. Page of Coins

The person will succeed in their initiatives, and these will have a fortunate outcome resulting in thriving circumstances for the person concerned.

1. Page of Cups
2. Page of Swords
3. Page of Wands

The justness of the person's cause combined with protection from powerful sources will cause them to win a major case.

1. Page of Cups
2. Page of Swords
3. Page of Coins

Bribery on the part of enemies and rivals will cause the person to lose a case, and this will damage their fortunes and peace of mind considerably.

1. Page of Wands
2. Page of Coins
3. Page of Cups

A legacy from a figure of great standing will provide the person with a pension that will enable them to live comfortably for the rest of their life.

1. Page of Wands
2. Page of Coins
3. Page of Swords

The person will lose a large gift on account of false friends.

1. Page of Wands
2. Page of Swords
3. Page of Cups

The querent will win the heart of a wealthy heiress, against her parents' wishes when he is least expecting it. This will result in his happiness and well-being.

1. Page of Wands
2. Page of Swords
3. Page of Coins

The person will gamble away a large sum, more than they can afford, and this will cause them to lose all credit with people.

1. Page of Wands
2. Page of Cups
3. Page of Coins

The person will receive an inheritance from a relative who lived abroad, and this will secure their well-being.

1. Page of Wands
2. Page of Cups
3. Page of Swords

A friend or relative will bequeath the person all their goods and chattels, and these will amount to a considerable inheritance.

1. Page of Coins
2. Page of Cups
3. Page of Wands

The person will make an advantageous marriage on account of their own good conduct. If already married they will be happy.

1. Page of Coins
2. Page of Cups
3. Page of Swords

The person will follow the advice of false friends, who will cause them to lose the proceeds of several years' work.

In a more general way, it is a warning to the querent to be wary.

1. Page of Coins
2. Page of Wands
3. Page of Cups

The person will be successful in love and in all their plans.

1. Page of Coins
2. Page of Wands
3. Page of Swords

A combination of indiscretion on the person's part and envy on the part of others will cause initiatives to fail.

1. Page of Coins
2. Page of Swords
3. Page of Cups

The person will not be most unlucky during their travels across water.

1. Page of Coins
2. Page of Swords
3. Page of Wands

The person will try to use force for illicit gain through an injustice of which they are well aware. This will cause them problems and expense, leaving matters in total disarray.

1. Page of Swords
2. Page of Cups
3. Page of Wands

The person will find a rogue friend in a foreign country, and the latter will return property they had stolen from them and with costs.

1. Page of Swords
2. Page of Cups
3. Page of Coins

The person will suffer two bankruptcies.

1. Page of Wands
2. Page of Wands
3. Page of Cups

The person will receive a valuable gift of jewellery.

1. Page of Swords
2. Page of Wands
3. Page of Coins

The person will lose a valuable piece of jewellery during the course of a journey.

1. Page of Swords
2. Page of Coins
3. Page of Cups

The person will lose their purse containing money through

their own imprudence, and this will cause them great problems.

1. Page of Swords
2. Page of Coins
3. Page of Wands

The person will lose the friendship of a benefactor for a while, and this will prove extremely detrimental to them.

THREE TENS

1. Ten of Cups
2. Ten of Coins
3. Ten of Wands

The person will succeed in a major business deal through the help of relatives and friends.

1. Ten of Cups
2. Ten of Coins
3. Ten of Swords

The effects of jealousy and enmity will cause the person to lose a deal, and this will prove most harmful to their fortunes.

1. Ten of Cups
2. Ten of Wands
3. Ten of Coins

In spite of envy on the part of others, the person will make a considerable sum of money from a business enterprise.

1. Ten of Cups
2. Ten of Wands
3. Ten of Swords

The person will win a large sum of money in a lottery.

1. Ten of Cups
2. Ten of Swords
3. Ten of Wands

The person will either win a case or earn a position as a result of their own talents, or else they will make a great deal of money in business. The circumstances of the person in question will be the decisive factor as regards which of the three things will happen to them.

1. Ten of Cups
2. Ten of Swords
3. Ten of Coins

The confidence the person places in friends will result in them being stripped of some of their property.

1. Ten of Wands
2. Ten of Coins
3. Ten of Cups

In spite of envy on the part of others, the person will return to a property or place of which they have been deprived.

1. Ten of Wands
2. Ten of Coins
3. Ten of Swords

The person will be unsuccessful in their initiatives or appointments despite having rightfully sought after them for a long time.

1. Ten of Wands
2. Ten of Swords
3. Ten of Cups

The person will make an extremely advantageous marriage with the help of relatives or loyal friends.

1. Ten of Wands
2. Ten of Swords
3. Ten of Coins

The effects of hatred and envy will rob the person of the opportunity of a good marriage or a firm foundation in life.

1. Ten of Wands
2. Ten of Cups
3. Ten of Coins

The person will find a valuable object.

1. Ten of Wands
2. Ten of Cups
3. Ten of Swords

Shortly before dying a relative or false friend will return an important item of property they had wrongly taken from the person.

1. Ten of Coins
2. Ten of Cups
3. Ten of Wands

Within a period of two years and a few months, following the death of a friend, the person will receive an inheritance that will give them much pleasure.

1. Ten of Coins
2. Ten of Cups
3. Ten of Swords

The person will be obliged to pay a debt they themselves have not contracted as a result of a sentence or on the advice of a friend.

1. Ten of Coins
2. Ten of Wands
3. Ten of Cups

In the course of the reading, the person will receive news and an item of property will unexpectedly be returned to them. This will be a source of great joy to them.

1. Ten of Coins
2. Ten of Wands
3. Ten of Swords

For some years the person will be preoccupied with matters stemming from bad faith on the part of friends or relatives.

1. Ten of Coins
2. Ten of Swords
3. Ten of Cups

A glaring injustice done to the person will reduce them to a state of melancholy.

1. Ten of Coins
2. Ten of Swords
3. Ten of Wands

The person will come up against a family matter that will cause them a great deal of sorrow.

1. Ten of Swords
2. Ten of Cups
3. Ten of Wands

The person will produce children who will make their life happy.

1. Ten of Swords
2. Ten of Cups
3. Ten of Coins

The person will lose a deal that would have secured their happiness, on account of having spoken openly and with confidence too soon.

1. Ten of Swords
2. Ten of Wands
3. Ten of Cups

With little money at their disposal, and through sheer hard work, the person will succeed in an affair that will secure their fortune and well-being for life.

1. Ten of Swords
2. Ten of Wands
3. Ten of Cups

The person will undertake a journey by sea, which will not go according to plan on account of their indiscretion regarding the state of their affairs.

1. Ten of Swords
2. Ten of Coins
3. Ten of Cups

The person will risk involvement in an enterprise in which their lack of knowledge will cost them their assets and their reputation.

1. Ten of Swords
2. Ten of Coins
3. Ten of Wands

The person is confident of an asset, but will be deprived of it when they least expect it as a result of hatred and envy.

Three Nines

1. Nine of Cups
2. Nine of Coins
3. Nine of Wands

In spite of envy on the part of others, through talent and hard work the person will earn enough money in a foreign country to keep them for the rest of their life.

1. Nine of Cups
2. Nine of Coins
3. Nine of Swords

The person will be deceived and most of their property will be stolen from them.

1. Nine of Cups
2. Nine of Wands
3. Nine of Coins

News of goods the person is to receive from a foreign country. The goods in question will open the way to happiness.

1. Nine of Cups
2. Nine of Wands
3. Nine of Swords

The person will gain property and honours in a foreign country.

1. Nine of Cups
2. Nine of Swords
3. Nine of Wands

The person will inherit a sizeable asset left to them by a relative living abroad.

1. Nine of Cups
2. Nine of Swords
3. Nine of Coins

The person will become a top-ranking dignitary in a foreign country, and occupy positions of great responsibility. Their path in this respect will prove hectic and stormy. However, acts of justice will make them persevere until the end of their days.

1. Nine of Wands
2. Nine of Coins
3. Nine of Cups

While in a foreign country the person will meet someone who is extremely wealthy, but prey to the utmost sorrow. Nevertheless they will find a way to give them back their happiness.

1. Nine of Wands
2. Nine of Coins
3. Nine of Swords

The person will be tricked by two foreigners/strangers.***

1. Nine of Wands
2. Nine of Swords
3. Nine of Cups

The person will have a major lottery win in a foreign country.

1. Nine of Wands
2. Nine of Swords
3. Nine of Coins

Foreign servants will steal personal effects and money from the person.

1. Nine of Wands
2. Nine of Cups
3. Nine of Coins

The person will discover a useful secret just when they least expect it.

1. Nine of Wands
2. Nine of Cups
3. Nine of Swords

The person will lose something valuable as a result of having acted with excessive haste, and this will give them cause for regrets.

1. Nine of Coins
2. Nine of Cups
3. Nine of Wands

The person will make something of a fortune in a foreign country, and this will secure their happiness and well-being for life.

1. Nine of Coins
2. Nine of Cups
3. Nine of Swords

The person will win the admiration of a great figure in a foreign country, thus their good fortune will be completely assured.

1. Nine of Coins
2. Nine of Wands
3. Nine of Cups

The person will gain property and inherited wealth in a foreign country.

*** Etranger can mean both "foreigner" and "stranger".

1. Nine of Coins
2. Nine of Wands
3. Nine of Swords

The person will lose inheritances or pensions in a foreign country after someone in whom they placed their trust acts in bad faith.

1. Nine of Coins
2. Nine of Swords
3. Nine of Cups

The person will lose something in a fire.

1. Nine of Coins
2. Nine of Swords
3. Nine of Wands

The person will lose a great deal of their possessions on account of water, but their fortunes will be restored within four years.

1. Nine of Swords
2. Nine of Cups
3. Nine of Wands

The death of several relatives will instantly improve the person's lot in life.

1. Nine of Swords
2. Nine of Cups
3. Nine of Coins

Death and illness will bring about great changes in the person's personal and material circumstances, and they will move to a foreign country to make good their losses.

1. Nine of Swords
2. Nine of Wands
3. Nine of Cups

Two rich and highly-esteemed persons will bring the person good fortune.

1. Nine of Swords
2. Nine of Wands
3. Nine of Coins

The person's own inconstancy in love combined with misplaced trust will cause them to lose a notable marriage.

1. Nine of Swords
2. Nine of Coins
3. Nine of Cups

The person will act as guarantor for two friends and will subsequently be obliged to pay on their behalf.

1. Nine of Swords
2. Nine of Coins
3. Nine of Wands

The person will lose court cases abroad on account of their own frivolous nature and inexperience in business.

Three Eights

1. Eight of Cups
2. Eight of Coins
3. Eight of Wands

Long life and unexpected prosperity.

1. Eight of Cups
2. Eight of Coins
3. Eight of Swords

Prosperity from personal successes.

1. Eight of Cups
2. Eight of Wands
3. Eight of Coins

The person will have a long life, and will be highly regarded and distinguished.

1. Eight of Cups
2. Eight of Wands
3. Eight of Swords

The person will triumph over enemies and will enjoy happiness, good fortune and contentment until the day they die.

1. Eight of Cups
2. Eight of Swords
3. Eight of Wands

Relatives or friends will come to the person's aid.

1. Eight of Cups
2. Eight of Swords
3. Eight of Coins

Your talents will attract envy on the part of others.

1. Eight of Wands
2. Eight of Coins
3. Eight of Cups

The person will make complete light of the envy and hatred directed at them by those wishing to spoil the honourable and lucrative circumstances in which they live.

1. Eight of Wands
2. Eight of Coins
3. Eight of Swords

The person will sometimes be troubled by false-hearted relatives or friends.

1. Eight of Wands
2. Eight of Swords
3. Eight of Cups

The person will be long lived and will receive legacies.

1. Eight of Wands
2. Eight of Swords
3. Eight of Coins

The person is ambitious, and this will lead to long drawn out business affairs

1. Eight of Wands
2. Eight of Cups
3. Eight of Coins

The person will be fortunate, in war, in love and in risky enterprises.

1. Eight of Wands
2. Eight of Cups
3. Eight of Swords

The person will be successful in their affairs or enterprises.

1. Eight of Coins
2. Eight of Cups
3. Eight of Wands

The person will marry a young woman of great breeding.

1. Eight of Coins
2. Eight of Cups
3. Eight of Swords

Long life full of social dissent.

1. Eight of Coins
2. Eight of Wands
3. Eight of Cups

The person will be fortunate in the company they keep, and people will trade with them both at sea and on land.

1. Eight of Coins
2. Eight of Wands
3. Eight of Swords

The person will lead a peaceful, tranquil life for a while, but soon their affairs will be troubled on account of bad conduct.

1. Eight of Coins
2. Eight of Swords
3. Eight of Cups

The person will have the presence of mind and courage to avoid the traps set for them by traitors.

1. Eight of Coins
2. Eight of Swords
3. Eight of Wands

The person will have good health and lead a most enjoyable life. All their initiatives will succeed, and they will watch their fortune grow.

1. Eight of Swords
2. Eight of Cups

3. Eight of Wands

The person's just nature combined with their talents will make them loved by all who deal with them.

1. Eight of Swords
2. Eight of Cups
3. Eight of Coins

The person will be appealing to others in both heart and mind.

1. Eight of Swords
2. Eight of Wands
3. Eight of Cups

A long wait and a long life full of hopes, which in the end will be happily fulfilled.

1. Eight of Swords
2. Eight of Wands
3. Eight of Coins

A long life, but this will not be welcome as the person will be afflicted by illness in old age.

1. Eight of Swords
2. Eight of Coins
3. Eight of Cups

The person will long enjoy the pleasures and satisfactions of the senses, and the consequences of this will prove dangerous.

1. Eight of Swords
2. Eight of Coins
3. Eight of Wands

Betrayal will cause the person no harm whatsoever, and the death of a relative will bring them good fortune.

Three Sevens

1. Seven of Cups
2. Seven of Coins
3. Seven of Wands

The person will grow lovesick, and the outcome will be a happy one.

1. Seven of Cups
2. Seven of Coins
3. Seven of Swords

The person will fall in love and become prey to jealousy. This obsession will pass with care and with the help of friends.

1. Seven of Cups
2. Seven of Wands
3. Seven of Coins

Envy and hatred projected by others will make the person ill. However, this illness will not last long.

1. Seven of Cups
2. Seven of Wands
3. Seven of Swords

The person will long enjoy the fruits of their labours. A brief illness will end their days.

1. Seven of Cups
2. Seven of Swords
3. Seven of Wands

The person will win the esteem, affection and heart of a well-to-do person who will make their life pleasant.

The protection of a person of rank will be in their favour in everything they do.

1. Seven of Cups
2. Seven of Swords
3. Seven of Coins

An ambition to acquire a great deal of possessions, will give the person cause to repent.

1. Seven of Wands
2. Seven of Coins
3. Seven of Swords

The person will be wounded in the service of their master, and the latter will compensate them for their infirmity by providing them with a pension.

1. Seven of Wands
2. Seven of Coins
3. Seven of Cups

The person will neglect their own affairs in order to oblige friends, who will then show their appreciation by displaying the most profound ingratitude.

1. Seven of Wands
2. Seven of Swords
3. Seven of Cups

The person will be saved from a shipwreck along with all their belongings by two faithful relatives or friends.

1. Seven of Wands
2. Seven of Swords
3. Seven of Coins

The person will gain from a fire. This gain can be explained in relation to the person's circumstances.

1. Seven of Wands
2. Seven of Cups
3. Seven of Coins

A dog will save the person's life by getting them out of the hands of a pair of would-be assassins.

1. Seven of Wands
2. Seven of Cups
3. Seven of Swords

One of the querent's friends will offer them money to ease their plight when they suffer a setback in their fortunes.
1. Seven of Coins
2. Seven of Cups
3. Seven of Wands

After a long struggle against poverty brought about by envy, the person will find themselves in a well-established position, which will bring them good fortune for the rest of their life.

1. Seven of Coins
2. Seven of Cups ****
3. Seven of Swords

Before marrying the person will suffer agony of mind.

1. Seven of Coins
2. Seven of Wands
3. Seven of Cups ****

A pregnancy will give the person cause for worry.
1. Seven of Coins
2. Seven of Swords
3. Seven of Cups

Through their own weakness the person will be greatly afflicted as a result of obsessive love.

1. Seven of Coins
2. Seven of Swords
3. Seven of Wands

The person will be made ill by bankruptcy.
1. Seven of Swords
2. Seven of Cups
3. Seven of Wands

After a long period of suffering the person will obtain the object of their desire.

1. Seven of Swords
2. Seven of Cups
3. Seven of Coins

The person will finally be granted the favours they desire, having long sighed for them in vain.

1. Seven of Swords
2. Seven of Wands
3. Seven of Cups

With the aid of money and friends, the person will gain satisfaction and prosperity from their trials and their labours.

**** The original says "Hearts"

1. Seven of Swords
2. Seven of Wands
3. Seven of Coins

The person will be out of work for a while on account of the disloyalty of two so-called friends.

1. Seven of Swords
2. Seven of Coins
3. Seven of Cups

The person will lose money at a game of chance as a result of the disloyalty of several friends.

1. Seven of Swords
2. Seven of Coins
3. Seven of Wands

The person will hardly ever win at games of chance. However on one occasion they will win a tidy sum.

THREE TWOS

1. Two of Cups
2. Two of Coins
3. Two of Wands

Meeting of relatives or well-intentioned friends aimed at helping the person with an initiative, which will subsequently prove successful.

1. Two of Cups
2. Two of Coins
3. Two of Swords

Meeting of false-hearted relatives or friends, who will blatantly betray the person. However, the latter will have satisfaction.

1. Two of Cups
2. Two of Wands
3. Two of Coins

The person will be betrayed by someone they thought was loyal. Time and patience will avenge them.

1. Two of Cups
2. Two of Wands
3. Two of Swords

With the help of a great personage and a friend, the person will take full revenge upon an enemy.

1. Two of Cups
2. Two of Swords
3. Two of Wands

With the aid of a loyal friend the person will discover an opening for their work, and this will fulfil their ambitions.

1. Two of Cups
2. Two of Swords
3. Two of Coins

The person will find out from

a friend that a false-hearted relative is envious of them, and will cast the relative out of their circle ignominiously.

1. Two of Wands
2. Two of Coins
3. Two of Cups

With the help of a friend, the person will regain the affection and protection of a great personage, having lost this as a result of the falsehoods recounted by someone envious of their good fortune.

1. Two of Wands
2. Two of Coins
3. Two of Swords

The person will be taken in by flatterers to such an extent that they will consequently do an injustice to two relatives or true friends.

1. Two of Wands
2. Two of Swords
3. Two of Cups

A friend who is deeply attached to the querent will reveal out of the goodness of their own heart that two false friends have hatched a criminal plot to rob them. The persons in question will not be allowed to gain the hoped-for advantage as the querent will be warned in time.

1. Two of Wands
2. Two of Swords
3. Two of Coins

A friend will take the person's side at a meeting, thus enabling them to triumph over the bad deeds of relatives, friends, enemies and those motivated by envy.

1. Two of Wands
2. Two of Cups
3. Two of Coins

A sincere friend will reveal envy on the part of someone the person had always regarded as their intimate. Knowing this will help the person them rid themselves of the culprit for life.

1. Two of Wands
2. Two of Cups
3. Two of Swords

The person catches out a friend in whom they had previously had complete confidence.

1. Two of Coins
2. Two of Cups
3. Two of Wands

The person will triumph over envy and its effects in the particular circumstances in which they find themselves.

1. Two of Coins
2. Two of Cups
3. Two of Swords

The person will lose some of their work, business or possessions as a result of envy and hatred.

1. Two of Coins
2. Two of Wands
3. Two of Cups

The person will be back in favour with relatives or friends, and the reconciliation will bring them many benefits from the persons in question.

1. Two of Coins
2. Two of Wands
3. Two of Swords

The person will lose a kind and faithful friend as a result of betrayal on the part of people they have obliged.

1. Two of Coins
2. Two of Swords
3. Two of Cups

A part of the person's worldly goods will come under attack, causing them some distress. However, they will be honoured by protection that will enable them to obtain restitution, compensation and damages.

1. Two of Coins
2. Two of Swords
3. Two of Wands

Envy will cause the person to become the enemy of their best friend, and they will have cause to repent of this.

1. Two of Swords
2. Two of Cups
3. Two of Wands

Thanks to a friend, the person will recover a debt that had driven them into bankruptcy.

1. Two of Swords
2. Two of Cups
3. Two of Wands

The person will lose property they had deposited with a trusted friend, and this will prove somewhat detrimental to them.

1. Two of Swords
2. Two of Wands
3. Two of Cups

The person will inherit money and real estate from their miserly relatives.

1. Two of Swords
2. Two of Wands
3. Two of Coins

The person is punished for their insolence having smeared

someone's reputation in the presence of a friend of theirs who springs to their defence.

1. Two of Swords
2. Two of Coins
3. Two of Cups

The person will be humiliated at a meeting by others who are motivated by envy.
1. Two of Swords
2. Two of Coins
3. Two of Wands

Trusted servants will steal valuable personal effects from the person.

THREE ACES

1. Ace of Cups
2. Ace of Coins
3. Ace of Wands

The person will win the esteem and confidence of a great personage, who will enhance their fortune.

1. Ace of Cups
2. Ace of Coins
3. Ace of Swords

The person will be deceived by a trusted friend, who will get rich at their expense.

1. Ace of Cups
2. Ace of Wands
3. Ace of Coins

The person will discover premeditated treachery on the part of false friends, and will provide mutual superiors with proof of this. The latter will treat the traitors with the utmost contempt and honour the person by giving them their confidence in the future.

1. Ace of Cups
2. Ace of Wands
3. Ace of Swords

A birth will bring the person joy and a wealth of possessions.

1. Ace of Cups
2. Ace of Swords
3. Ace of Wands

By chance the person will gain the esteem of a sovereign, who will make them rich and respectable.

1. Ace of Cups
2. Ace of Swords
3. Ace of Coins

A fortunate encounter with destiny in a wood or garden will lead to the person spending some happy days during the course of their lifetime.

1. Ace of Wands
2. Ace of Coins
3. Ace of Cups

With the help of true friends, many things will go in the person's favour.

1. Ace of Wands
2. Ace of Coins
3. Ace of Swords

The person will find no happiness in either love or friendship.

1. Ace of Wands
2. Ace of Swords
3. Ace of Cups

The person will be loved by all those they frequent, and will benefit from this.

1. Ace of Wands
2. Ace of Swords
3. Ace of Coins

Money the person lent without interest will be repaid with ingratitude.

1. Ace of Wands
2. Ace of Cups
3. Ace of Coins

The person will win a huge sum of money in a lottery.

1. Ace of Wands
2. Ace of Cups
3. Ace of Swords

The querent will shower a young person with gifts, thus winning their heart. This will bring them joy, plus an essential service at a time of urgent need.

1. Ace of Coins
2. Ace of Cups
3. Ace of Wands

The person will inherit a sum of money and numerous items which will make their initiatives fruitful.

1. Ace of Coins
2. Ace of Cups
3. Ace of Swords

The person will be cruelly attacked by relatives or associates out of self-interest or envy.

1. Ace of Coins
2. Ace of Wands
3. Ace of Cups

Honour and justice will be

done to the person, and benefits will ensue, with elevation to high places, fortune and honours of all kinds.

1. Ace of Coins
2. Ace of Wands
3. Ace of Swords

The sincere friendship of a woman will arouse envy in others, who will then set fire to the person's house. The faithful friend will be the one to rescue them from this incident.

1. Ace of Coins
2. Ace of Swords
3. Ace of Cups

Self-interest and ingratitude on the part of supposed friends will render the person's work fruitless for a while. However, in numerous cases, assuming the burden of such painful matters and handling them with a combination of courage and patience will cause them to triumph.

1. Ace of Coins
2. Ace of Swords
3. Ace of Wands

Good news about an inheritance the person had been deprived of for some time.

1. Ace of Swords
2. Ace of Cups
3. Ace of Wands

The person will earnestly seek better circumstances than their current ones. Their quest will be a complete success.

1. Ace of Swords
2. Ace of Cups
3. Ace of Coins

The person will entrust goods to two other people, and will consequently be cheated out of a major portion of them.

1. Ace of Swords
2. Ace of Wands
3. Ace of Cups

The person will have satisfaction regarding an injustice that has caused them a great deal of trouble. This, combined with major gains, will re-establish the person honourably.

1. Ace of Swords
2. Ace of Wands
3. Ace of Coins

The effects of false relationships will cause the person bitter sorrow.

1. Ace of Swords
2. Ace of Coins
3. Ace of Cups

Being naturally good and kind, the person will enhance the circumstances of others, perhaps even in excess of their expectations. For the most part they will be repaid with ingratitude.

1. Ace of Swords
2. Ace of Coins
3. Ace of Wands

The person will arouse the envy of others on account of their talents, merits and services rendered. They will suffer a few humiliations, but these will be erased by justice and reason.

CHAPTER FIVE

Interplay of the arcana and numbers

Cartomancers wishing to discover all the secrets of the Tarot, and even philosophers wishing to consult this ancient book of primitive sciences, must bear in mind that the combination of hieroglyphics and numbers gives some exceedingly valuable indications.

Therefore, I would advise any true practitioner to make an enlarged reproduction of the table above which represents the three aspects of each of the 12 astrological houses. Any Tarot card falling into one of these 36 boxes takes on new meanings, and these can be invaluable in case of doubt. All in-depth study of cartomancy should culminate in the use of this astrological table.

Mademoiselle Lenormand made great use of the astrological table, but hers was square, and unlike the Egyptian one, which I have reconstituted in its original form, it did not show the duodenary table relationships.

However, since certain writers copy the research of original authors without quoting their sources, I have left a slight error in this table, which will not be at all detrimental to the divinatory meaning, but will make it possible to expose any plagiarist straight away.

Number 1, Plans

- A Cup card** in position number 1 means felicitous success with plans. The three accompanying cards will give fuller information on events if consulted separately.
- A Wand in space 1 marked "plans" indicates that trustworthy people will do all they can to make sure plans succeed.
- A Coin in space 1 means the person will be up against enormous problems with their affairs as a result of envy on the part of others, and the accompanying cards will reveal the causes of the delay or failure.
- A Sword in this space means betrayal, and the outlook for the person is poor.

Number 2, Satisfaction

- Heaven will look favourably upon the person's wishes and these will be fulfilled if there is a Cup in space 2, marked. The accompanying cards will give information about effects, events etc.
- A Wand in space 2 is an indication that fidelity will overcome all and will make the querent happy. The three accompanying cards will explain the circumstances.
- A Coin in space 2 indicates great problems with envy, which must be overcome. The three accompanying cards will show the reasons for the delay.
- A Sword in space 2 means betrayal and little cause for hope.

** The type of card is not specified here, but given the text that follows the reference has to be to a "Cup" card.

INTERPLAY OF THE ARCANA AND NUMBERS 229

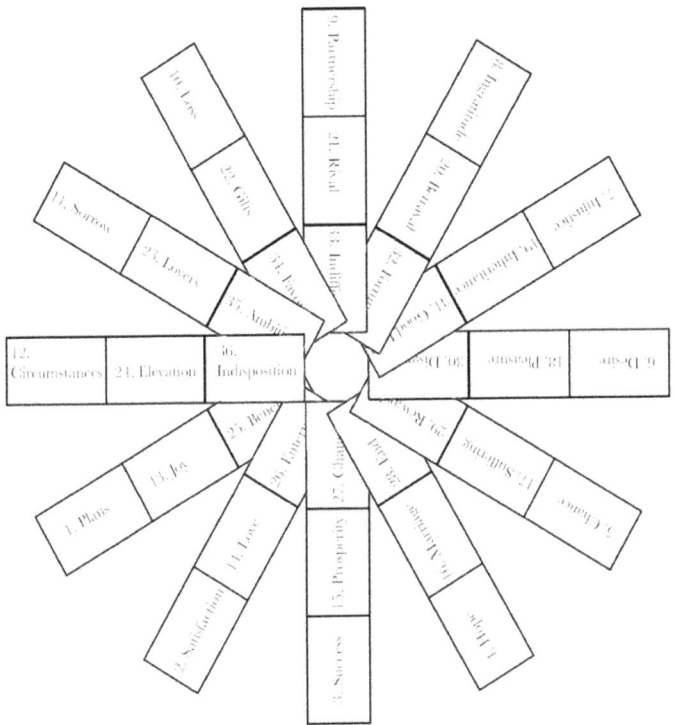

THE ASTROLOGICAL TABLE

NUMBER 3, SUCCESS

In this case the word success should be interpreted in the light of the person's circumstances and the nature of their affairs.

A Cup in space 3 denotes success of an extremely favourable kind. The three accompanying cards will give a more detailed explanation of the reasons for this if consulted according to their individual values.

A Wand in space 3 means that, with the help of friends, the person will succeed and will keep the envy and jealousy of others at bay. For a fuller explanation consult the three accompanying cards.

- A Coin in space 3 means that the person will have many difficulties to overcome, and will enjoy little success in their initiatives even if they fulfil their duties with honour.
- A Sword is a forewarning to the querent that they will be betrayed, and this will prevent them from succeeding in their plans. More information on this will be contained in the three accompanying cards.

Number 4, Hope

- A Cup card in space 4 means that the person's hopes will be crowned with good fortune, success and fulfilment. The three accompanying cards will give further information on the events in question.
- A Wand means that through their own efforts and with the help of their friends, all the person's hopes will be fulfilled.
- A Coin in space 4 signifies and represents hopes that have little foundation and that will be completely in vain.
- A Sword in this space heralds hopes that are ill-conceived or that are wrecked through and through on account of betrayal. The three other cards will give more information on the matter.

Number 5, Chance

Chance should be understood to mean a win in a lottery or at cards or other games of chance, persons who become lovers, benefactors or thieves, or else losses caused by fire or water.

- A Cup in space 5 indicates that luck will smile upon the person, thus making their fortune and placing them in a highly esteemed position. The three accompanying cards will provide more detailed information.
- A Wand in space 5 is an indication to the person that, with the help of friends or benefactors, fate will put them within reach of trying to achieve a better lot in life, and that they will be highly successful in their attempt.
- A Coin in this position is a sign to the person that fate will procure them a lover, a benefactor, a prosperous journey, an inheritance or news of relatives. The three accompanying cards, examined in conjunction with the card in 17 and its four accompanying cards

INTERPLAY OF THE ARCANA AND NUMBERS   231

read according to both their individual and combined meanings indicate that Cups*** should be interpreted as good relatives, Wands as faithful friends, Coins as things foreign and Swords as bad relatives or friends who bode ill. In other words, if there are Swords in space 5, these will mean bad luck such as theft, bankruptcy and loss caused by fire or water.

NUMBER 6, DESIRE****

The verb and the object, to desire and desire, should be taken to mean money, mistress or lover, succession, inheritance, association, possession, marriage, discoveries and talents.

A Cup in space 6 means the person will see their burning desire fulfilled.

A Coin in this space means that for the time being it is necessary to suppress envy and appease interested persons in order to obtain the object of one's desire.

A Sword in space 6 is an indication to the person that their desire will not be fulfilled.

The three accompanying cards will give further information on all these events, whether in the case of Swords, Coins, Wands or Cups.

NUMBER 7, INJUSTICE

The word injustice should be applied to things that are undeserved, such as loss of a position or legal case, or losing the esteem of benefactors on account of falsehoods or misinterpretation in matters of trust.

In this case, if a Cup is in space 7 then the injustice done to the person will be remedied to their complete satisfaction. For fuller information consult the three accompanying cards.

A Wand in space 7 indicates that the person must pull all possible strings with their friends in order for honour to be redressed. This will depend on the justice of their request. In order to discover whether the outcome is a happy one, consult the three accompanying cards.

*** The original edition has this as 'Hearts'
**** The Wands are missing in the original edition

A Coin in space 7 is a forewarning that the person will have to resort to presents in order to obtain honourable reparation for an injustice that has been done to them. Consult the three accompanying cards for indications regarding these future events.

A Sword in space 7 means that nothing could erase the injustice that has been done to the person, and in order to prevent the injustice from escalating they must keep quiet and pretend to forget it.

Number 8, Ingratitude****

Ingratitude [and thankless tasks] have their causes, both natural and forced. For example, a person might lend money to someone who is powerless to pay it back, and then have to demand repayment harshly or via legal means. Or, out of the goodness of their heart, they might employ a man who does not keep faith with others, thus giving him an opportunity to act ungratefully by putting him in a position to be able to harm them.

In other words, we should never complain about how ungrateful people are, as it is often we ourselves who provide them with the opportunity for this by placing too much trust in them.****

A Cup in space 8 means the person will obtain ample justice with regard to persons who have disobliged them through ingratitude.

A Coin in this space is an indication to the person that envy will be the sole cause of the ingratitude with which they are repaid.

A Sword in space 8 means that the person will be betrayed by the very people they have obliged to a considerable degree, and that in order to avoid further problems, they must pretend to be impervious to this, keep quiet and even do good to these ungrateful people.

In the case of all the instances quoted above, further detail will be provided by the three accompanying cards.

Number 9, Partnership

A Cup card in space 9 is an indication to the person that all their partnerships will succeed in accordance with their wishes.

**** The Wands are missing in the original edition

A Wand in space 9 means that, with hard work and help from friends, partnerships will grow fruitful.

A Coin in space 9 indicates that envy will cause the person's partnerships to suffer.

A Sword in space 9 means that the partner or associate will bring good fortune to others, but not to the querent.

The three accompanying cards will provide fuller information.

The word partnership is intended to refer to all events such as marriage, trading, manufacturing and entrepreneurial partnerships and companionship at arms and in the smuggling trade, depending upon the circumstances and hopes of the person for whom you are drawing the cards.

Number 10, Loss

A Cup in space 10 is an indication to the person that they will lose benefactors and that they will feel the loss greatly.

A Wand in this space means that the person will lose faithful friends, and their hopes will be dashed in the process.

A Coin in space 10 is an indication to the person that they will suffer a material loss, i.e. money, land, a legacy or a legitimate claim, furniture, jewellery etc….

A Sword in this space means the person will suffer a major loss in terms of business interests. Consult the four accompanying cards, and these will inform you of the nature of the loss.

Number 11, Sorrow

A Cup in space 11 means that the person will suffer bitter sorrow brought on by love or by their own family.

A Wand in space 11 represents sorrow in connection with friendships.

A Coin in this space heralds troubled times for the person's business interests. The accompanying cards will explain the nature of these problems.

A Sword in space 11 means that the person will suffer vexations brought on by jealousy and betrayal.

Number 12, Circumstances

A Cup in space 12 means the person's circumstances will improve daily.

A Wand in this space means the person's circumstances will be enhanced and that with perseverance, hard work and the help of faithful friends, they will prosper.

A Coin in space 12 is a forewarning to the person that, as a result of envy, they will be stuck in a difficult position.

A Sword in this space means a deterioration in circumstances. Note that these future circumstances will only last for the length of time foretold by the spread.

Number 13, Joy

A Cup in space 13 means the person will experience pure joy that is not only pleasurable but highly profitable.

A Wand in this space is an indication to the person that they will increase their fortune through the services of faithful friends.

A Coin in space 13 means that the person will experience the joy and thrill of triumphing in a business matter despite envy on the part of others.

A Sword in this space means the person will be overjoyed at having been of help to their superiors, who will then increase their fortune.

Number 14, Love

A Cup in space 14 means the person will find happiness in love.

A Wand in this space means the person will find fidelity in love.

A Coin in space 14 means love marred by jealousy.

A Sword in this space means the person's love will be betrayed. The four accompanying cards will provide information as to such events.

Number 15, Prosperity

A Cup in space 15 heralds prosperity for the person through legitimate means.

A Wand in this space means that through their own intelligence and shrewdness and with the help of faithful friends, the person will make more than enough to constitute an honest living within their given circumstances.

A Coin in space 15 heralds a decline in the person's fortunes as a result of envy.

A Sword in this space means that the effects of hatred and ill-faith will destroy the prosperity of the person for whom one is drawing the cards.

Number 16, Marriage

The reading should be about marriage if the person is of marriageable age. If not, or if the person is already married, then number 16 should be taken to pertain to close relatives or benefactors, because the effects of good or of bad events must be relevant to the person for whom you are drawing the cards.

A Cup in space 16 heralds mutual love and therefore a happy marriage for the person concerned.

A Wand in this space means that, with the help of friends, the person will secure an agreeable marriage to a wealthy partner.

A Coin in space 16 is a forewarning to the person that their marriage will be marred by jealousy.

A Sword in this space means that betrayal and envy will cause the person to lose an opportunity to marry a person of means.

Number 17, Suffering

A Cup in space 17 is a forewarning to the person that they will suffer an affliction of the heart, but this will not last very long.

A Wand in this space means the person will suffer on account of a friend, and only reconciliation will erase the problem.

A Coin in space 17 means the person will suffer the effects of envy.

A Sword in this space represents considerable suffering for the person on account of a betrayal.

Number 18, Pleasure

A Cup in space 18 indicates that the person's love affairs will be full of mutual desires and pleasure untainted with bitterness.

A Wand in this space means that, through their own attentiveness and courteous gestures, and with the help of friends, the person will win the heart of their mistress or lover, and their feelings will be returned.

A Coin in space 18 denotes that pleasures will be stormy and troubled by the effects of jealousy, but in the end matters will be resolved without any seriously unpleasant incidents.

A Sword in this space indicates that pleasures are likely to be interrupted and of short duration.

Number 19, Inheritance

A Cup in space 19 indicates that the person will receive a legitimate inheritance of considerable size.

A Wand in this space means that friends of the querent will leave them a share of their belongings.

A Coin in space 19 indicates that envy and the interests of false relatives or friends will cause the person to lose a large part of a legitimate inheritance.

A Sword in this space indicates that an act of betrayal will cause the person to lose an item of inherited property or a donation bequeathed by a benefactor.

Number 20, Betrayal

A Cup in space 20 is an indication to the person that, although others will betray them, the harm the traitors wished to inflict will rebound upon themselves.

A Wand in this space means that, with the help of faithful friends, the person will be saved from a major act of betrayal that would have disrupted their affairs completely.

A Coin in space 20 is a forewarning that the person will suffer a betrayal as a result of envy. This will upset them greatly, but all will pass with time.

A Sword in this space means that the person's hopes will be betrayed as a result of slander, and that they will consequently lose friends.

Number 21, Rival

In love the word rival should be taken to refer to a lover or mistress, and in matters of property, an item to which the person lays concurrent claim.

A Cup in space 21 indicates that the person will have preference over their rivals, and all manner of satisfaction will derive from this.

A Wand in this space is an indication to the person that their personal merit, together with the good offices of true friends will win them victory over their rivals.

A Coin in space 21 means that, through jealousy and intrigue, the person's rivals will win some of the favours they themselves are soliciting.

A Sword in this space indicates a complete fall from grace for the person concerned, with all favours granted to their rivals.

Number 22, Gifts

A Cup in space 22 means that the person will receive valuable gifts over and above their expectations.

A Wand in this space indicates significant gifts given to the person in a spirit of amour propre.

A Coin in space 22 represents a vile, low, contemptible heart that can be won over with the smallest of gifts.

A Sword in this space heralds treacherous gifts from a person acting out of evil intentions in order to allay the suspicions the person would be quite right to have against them.

Number 23, Lovers

A Cup in space 23 indicates that the person will have a lover or mistress of good character, who will be deeply attached to them. The same interpretation applies to friends.

A Wand in this space represents a lover or mistress who is faithful and of good breeding, and who is disposed towards doing right by the person concerned. The same interpretation applies to friends.

A Coin in space 23 is a forewarning that the person will have a lover or mistress who is prone to jealousy, and who will cause problems with their suspicions and their sullenness. It also means the person will have jealous, touchy, self-interested friends.

A Sword in this space is a forewarning that the person will have a mistress or lover who is cunning, self-interested, vindictive and fickle. The same interpretation applies in the case of a friend.

Number 24, Elevation

"Elevation" must be regarded as lucky chance, even though this is predestined to happen to the person concerned.

A Cup in space 24 indicates that the person will be elevated to a station far above their expectations, and that they will be admired and esteemed by respectable citizens.

A Wand in this space indicates that through scrupulous attention to duty, and with the help of loyal friends, the person will obtain both elevated status and wealth.

A Coin in space 24 tells the person that envy on the part of others will delay their rise for a considerable length of time.

A Sword in this space is a forewarning to the person that disloyalty on the part of others will constantly spoil their chances of elevation.

Number 25, Well-Deserved Benefits

A Cup in space 25 indicates that the person will receive well-deserved recompense as expected or as promised by their superiors.

A Wand in this space means that, with the help of friends, the person will receive the benefits they deserve.

A Coin in space 25 indicates that, on account of envy, the person will have a great deal of trouble gaining recognition of their claim to the benefits they justly deserve, and will only receive part of them.

A Sword in this space is an indication to the person concerned that the benefits they deserve will be given to another as a result of a betrayal.

Number 26, Enterprise

A Cup in space 26 is an indication to the person that all their enterprises will be blessed with good fortune.

A Wand in this space means that the person will receive help from friends in all their initiatives, and that these will be lucrative.

A Coin in space 26 means that the person will be plagued by envy and self-interest on the part of others, and such factors will mar the success of their enterprises greatly.

A Sword in this space is a forewarning that the majority of the person's enterprises will be to their disadvantage, that is to say enterprises undertaken with a view to procuring a rapid increase in wealth, not those that serve to provide the basic necessities of life.

Number 27, Change

A Cup in space 27 is an indication to the person that they will undergo a fortunate change in terms of wealth and honours.

A Wand in this space means that, with the help of loyal friends, the person will achieve a change of circumstances and fortune.

A Coin in space 27 is an indication to the person concerned that the effects of envy will alter their position to their disadvantage.

A Sword in this space means that the person will experience no change in their circumstances.

Number 28, Death and End

A Cup in space 28 means that the death of a relative or benefactor will increase the fortune of the person for whom you are drawing the horoscope.

A Wand in this space is an indication to the person that a friend will leave them something of benefit to remember them by.

A Coin in space 28 heralds the death of one of the querent's enemies.

A Sword in this space heralds the death of the person who has caused the querent the most harm during their lifetime.

Number 29, Rewards

A Cup in space 29 means that the person will be rewarded with kindness for their industry, work, fidelity or devotion and that they will be held in high esteem.

A Wand in space 29 is an indication that, through the offices of friends, the person will receive the reward due to them, and in which they have placed all their hopes.

A Coin in space 29 is a forewarning to the person that envy on the part of others will delay their reward, or rather will decrease it.

A Sword in this space means the person will suffer a betrayal, and this will result in loss of a promised or expected reward.

Number 30, Fall from Grace

A Cup in space 30 is an indication to the person that they will suffer a fall from grace, but will have no difficulty putting this behind them.

A Wand in this space means one of the person's friends or benefactors will suffer a fall from grace, and this will affect them.

A Coin in space 30 is a forewarning that the effects of envy will cause the person to be out of favour in ways they will find noticeable.

A Sword in this space means that a trusted friend of the querent will betray them, thus causing them to be out of favour with a number of people.

Number 31, Good Luck

A Cup in space 31 means the person will have an unexpected stroke of luck that will make life pleasant for them.

A Wand in this space is an indication that, with the help of friends, the person will benefit from a stroke of luck, and this will increase their fortune considerably.

A Coin in space 31 is an indication that the effects of envy and ambition on the part of false friends will work in the querent's favour.

A Sword in this space is an indication that the person will he helped by friends in a situation of urgent need. That is to say, an attempt will be made on the querent's life, and the killer who is threatening them will be turned aside by friends. Any method including poison will be used to destroy the querent, but to no avail.

NUMBER 32, FORTUNE

A Cup in space 32 is an indication to the person that they will make their fortune brilliantly, and in full accordance with their expectations.

A Wand in this space indicates that, by dint of their own effort and intelligence, and with some help from true and beneficent friends, the querent will make their fortune.

A Coin in space 32 is a forewarning that envious individuals in whom too much confidence has been placed will make their fortune at the querent's expense, finding ingenious ways of taking advantage of their excessive good nature.

A Sword in this space is an indication to the person that all their talent and hard work will serve only to make the fortunes of traitors who come ostensibly to serve them, and the fruits of their entitlement will merely enable them to remain at a standstill, in other words at subsistence level. See the three accompanying cards.

NUMBER 33, INDIFFERENCE

A Cup in space 33 is a sign to the person that their indifference to the welfare of others will bring them a period of tranquillity.

A Wand in this space is an indication to the person that their indifference with regard to their choice of friends will frequently cause them grief.

A Coin or a Sword in space 33 is an indication to the person that they will lose good opportunities through their indifference, and that others who are more mindful and vigilant than they are will reap what they have overlooked. Consult the three accompanying cards.

NUMBER 34, FAVOUR

A Cup in space 34 means that the person will obtain favours in love and will earn the consideration of rich persons who will make their fortune.

A Wand in this space is an indication to the person that their wise and edifying conduct will win them all their causes.

A Coin in space 34 is an indication that the person will have great difficulty obtaining any real favours.

A Sword in this space means that the person will solicit fruitful favours in vain.

See the three accompanying cards.

Number 35, Ambition

A Cup in space 35 means the person can expect their ambitions to be totally fulfilled, and that these will bring the desired result.

A Wand in this space is an indication that through their own merit and intelligence in choosing friends, all the querent's ambitions in connection with their circumstances and hopes will succeed to their liking.

A Coin in space 35 is a forewarning to the person that jealousy on the part of friends, associates and relatives will alter and delay their prospects of fulfilling their ambitions.

A Sword in this space means that the person will be deprived of the chief object of their ambitions on account of the shrewdness and disloyalty of friends. See the three accompanying cards.

Number 36, Indisposition

The illnesses will be short if there is a Cup in space 36. If a Wand is there they will not be serious. If a Sword is there the illnesses can only attack your enemies. If a Coin is there, a slight indisposition will cause you to miss a pleasure trip.

CHAPTER SIX

General conclusion

Revered masters, initiators of Ancient Egypt, it is the Mountebank, the conjurer, the entertainer you have placed at the start of your book of eternal science.

Once, initiates were given a clay beetle with a hidden spring fastening, which opened it to reveal the twelve Gods of Mount Olympus sculpted in gold and ivory. The Tarot should be presented in much the same way.

The conjurer introduces himself to all snobs and pedants who despise the topic of fortune-telling when presenting the teachings of Occult Science and says: "See my cup-shaped shakers, my sword, my talismans. I entertain the crowds, I teach sages. But you teach nothing unless you entertain".

That is why, revered masters, before following the path already illustrated by Guillaume Postel and Raymond Lull before him, and by Dr Eliphas Levi, and before that by the intuitive, Etteilla; before talking about the deck as a whole from a philosophical and religious point of view, I want to describe the Tarot of the Mountebank, of the cartomancer, that admirable book of the vendor of hopes. Everything in the natural world has its own coherence, and whilst the Mountebank, who opens the book, is surrounded by the physical instruments of magic, Truth, which closes the book, unfolds between the four symbols of the live forces in action on all planes. In the same way, philosophical Tarot is both an end and a complement to divinatory Tarot, which in turn provides the introduction.

That is why, revered masters, I whose book is the issue of your teachings, humbly dedicate my modest work to you and to your memory, and ask you to give your blessing to those who understand it and pardon those who mock it, because they do not understand it.

If you look exclusively at the period up until 1880, there were four main contemporaries working on the Tarot, namely Etteilla, d'Odoucet, Eliphas Lévi and Christian. I intend to give an outline of the research carried out by Etteilla and Eliphas Levi. As far as the work of d'Odoucet and Christian are concerned, a look at the earlier Chapter II will suffice.

Etteilla

Etteilla studied the numbers and hieroglyphs of Tarot. Let me give a couple of examples of his research into the Book of Thoth from a numerical point of view.

Drawing Tarot Cards

Ignorant people always operate badly in everything they do, but the same is not true of educated people. Thus the Egyptians took the Book of Thoth, shuffled it in every way without looking at the Hieroglyphics. Then they told their querents to cut the deck in two, took the first card and put it in position B, the second in position A and the third in B again (i.e. B, A). They then put the fourth card in B, the fifth in A and the sixth in B, then the seventh in B and so on until the end, so that there are twenty-six cards on pile A and fifty-two cards on pile B.

Next they would take the pile of fifty-two and repeat the same process to form piles C and D, in such a way that the C pile contained 17 cards and the D pile 35 cards. They then put the seventeen cards aside and repeated the whole process using the remaining pile of thirty-five, thus forming piles F and E, in which pile E contained eleven cards and pile F twenty-four cards.

Thus A = 26, B = 0, C = 17, D = 0, E = 11, F = 24, but the last of these piles was not read. (Note that, before each stage of the operation, it is necessary to shuffle the cards and cut them.)

And so, taking pile A, they would read one card at a time, going from right to left, the spirit of the reading being entirely due to its individual parts. Then they would take the first card and read it in relation to the twenty-sixth. Lastly, they interpreted piles C and E.

Read the third edition of *Cartomancie*, published in 1782, and it will give you the whole procedure. Although, I have to admit that Etteilla's work was no more than a copy after the style of the Egyptians, as was Steganography by Trithemius. I would say Raymond Lull's theory too was a copy of the Book of Thoth, or to put it more plainly, of the cards called the Tarot.

Their second procedure was to draw three times 7 cards, and arrange these as follows:

7.6.5.4.3.2.1. A.
7.6.5.4.3.2.1. B.
7.6.5.4.3.2.1. C.

If A did not answer their questions they would place another 7 cards underneath: 7.6.5.4.3.2.1. If this still did not provide any answers, they would draw another 7 cards, 7.6.5.4.3.2.1. A through to C if they still had not found a solution or a positive prognosis. If all these repetitions said nothing, then they would advise their querents to pray to the gods, to alter the way they handled things and to come back the next day or several days later.

Their third procedure was of considerable scope and called for considerable thought. Having shuffled and cut the 78 cards, they would lay them out in a form resembling two columns with a capital laid across the top. Then, without reshuffling the cards, they would make a circle, taking care to remove the 1st card or the 8th, depending on the sex of the querent. When this first or eighth hieroglyph turned up, they would place it in the middle as illustrated in the figure below.

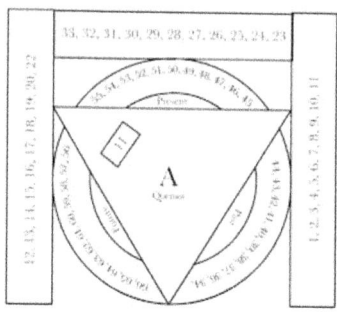

They would place the first card they drew in position 1, and so on up till 11. They would then put the 12th card in position 12, and so on up until 22 etc. ...

1 to 11 and 34 to 44 represented the past; 12 to 22 and 45 to 55. represented the future and 23 to 33 and 56 to 66 represented the present.

If the 1 or the 8 did not appear—depending on the sex of the querent—they would remove the relevant card from the remainder of the deck and place it in the middle as illustrated, no. 8, supposing that the spread is for a woman. No. 1 would be for a man, because the distance between a man and a woman is seven degrees. That was what caused Mohammed to make a mistake when he said that women are houris, who will not enter Paradise but will guard the door. He did not understand that this difference of seven degrees only exists in the physical world.

The Egyptians used to read all the sections one after the other, explaining first the past, then the present, then the future. So they would take 8, 34 and 1 to represent the past and continue with this procedure until they got up to 8, 44 and 11, and the same went for the present and the future. I think it is necessary to read Etteilla if you wish to understand how to read this spread, three cards in relation to one another and always using the middle card.

Sometimes, Egyptian sages would begin their readings with 12 cards. But that was always for the purposes of major things such as harvests, decisions, battles, or for the rulers of the land or of foreign lands, or for their constituents. But having completed the three procedures I describe above, they would do a fourth, or even a fifth or a sixth if they wished or if the numbers directed them to. For example: when drawing the cards, if they saw a number that was particularly well or badly placed in relation to the rest, they would make a mental note of it, and when they had finished drawing the cards, they would draw as many cards as the well or badly-placed card indicated to them.

If it so happened that a man had only one question to ask, and it was a legitimate one—for they were against all that smacked of wrongdoing or that might lead to such—they would simply draw five cards: e.d.c.b.a., going from right to left as usual. If that brought no answer, they would draw ten more cards and arrange them thus:

5 .4. 3. 2. 1.
E. D. C .B. A.
10. 9. 8. 7. 6.

They would read the cards, going from 1 to 5, from A to E and from 6 to 10. Then, as I explained before, if the cards still said nothing, they told the querent to come back another day, and to worship the gods ever more strongly and love their fellow human beings or their neighbour.

I could subject the whole of the Book of Thoth, as divided into books 1,2,3,4,5,6 and 7 to huge amounts of calculations, and the code thus obtained would show me the formula and give me all the keys. But here is a table that will provide a starting point for those wishing to do an in-depth general interpretation of the Book of Thoth.

Note first of all that 1, or unity, progresses to 10, 2 to 13, 3 to 16, 4 to 12, 5 to 8, 6 to 11 and 7 to 14.

Order, harmony and the utmost concordance reigns in all these numbers, partly because they agree and partly because the agent is attentive to the patient as in 6 to 11. But in general, the best way to explain is to say that there are 7 distinct tones or degrees in the 7 chains of the alphabet and the formulae. The number 2, which is central to the formula, relates to 13. I pointed out that according to philosophers this number was weak, that it readily assumed lesser importance than the seven numbers that followed. But it was the two that gave them their flow, their movement and lastly the orders of unity. It is the zealous minister to 1 and the faithful friend of 3, which is the king of numbers, not including unity. Lastly, 2 is the second divisor of the perfect number 6 and is concurrent with 3. 6 signals sin, and in a way its opposite, for sin here is to be understood as weakness. It is also close to 2. It supports the weight of 13, of which 2 is the custodian or guard. Not that this weight is unnatural. It is simply burdensome, for death is a state of perfection, even though it is one of the greatest signs of weakness. But it is perfection alone that tends towards regeneration, as Pythagoras clearly realised.

Eliphas Lévi

Eliphas Lévi is one of the writers who has pursued the study of all aspects of Tarot to the fullest extent. I have many manuscripts by this author, and am going to give my readers the benefit of a few unusual items.

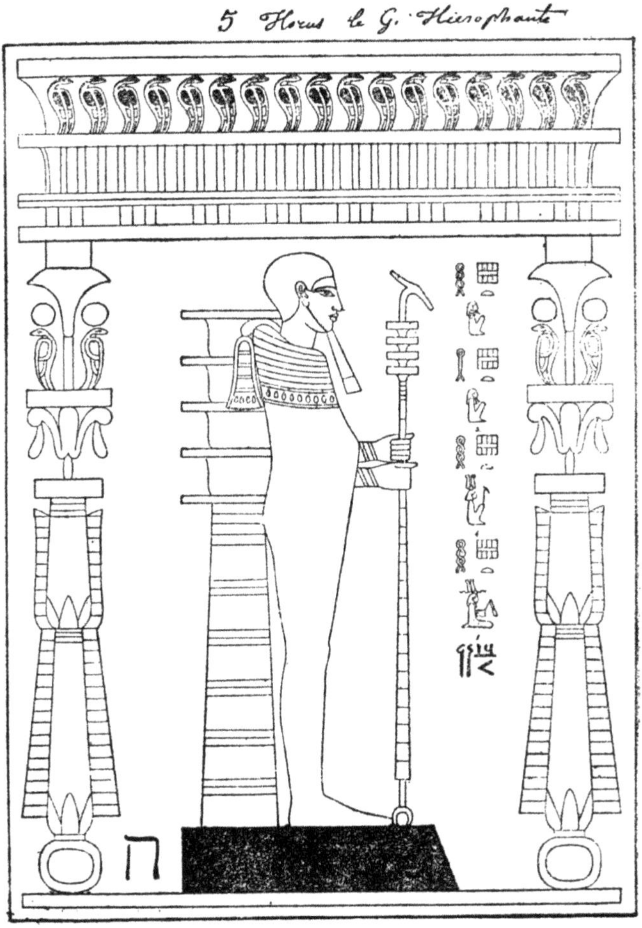

GENERAL CONCLUSION 249

5 Horus le G. Hierophante

UNPUBLISHED DOCUMENTS OF ELIPHAS LEVI ABOUT THE TAROT

250 THE DIVINATORY TAROT

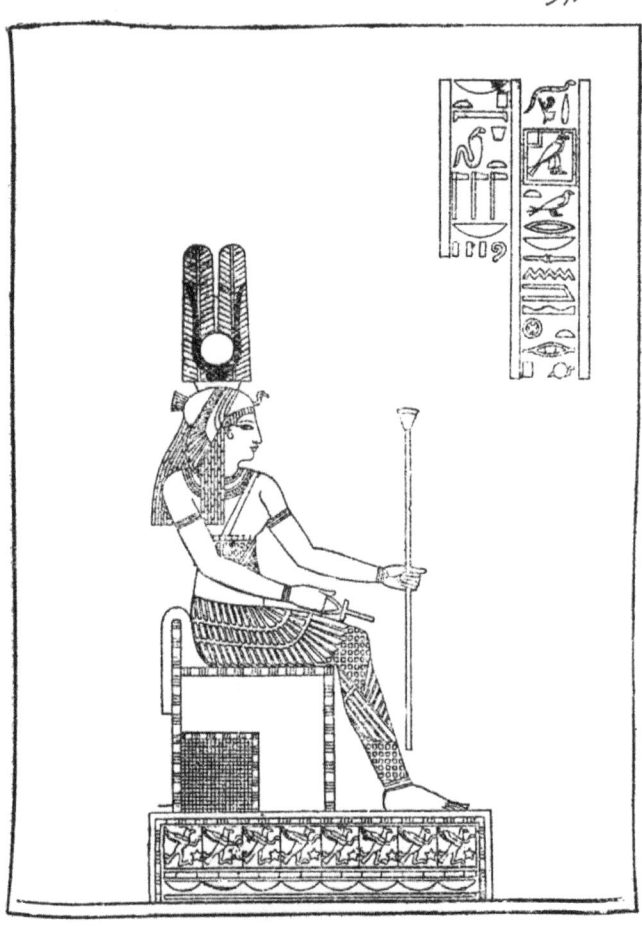

UNPUBLISHED DOCUMENTS OF ELIPHAS LEVI ABOUT THE TAROT
(The notes on the page are the hand writing of Eliphas Levi)

INDIAN TAROT
The Third Incarnation of Vishnu

INDIAN TAROT
The Tenth Incarnation of Vishnu

INDIAN TAROT
The Seventh Incarnation of Vishnu

INDIAN TAROT
The Ninth Incarnation of Vishnu

GENERAL CONCLUSION 255

INDIAN TAROT
The Fourth Incarnation of Vishnu